V&R

Margit Ernst-Habib

But Why Are You Called a Christian?

An Introduction to the
Heidelberg Catechism

Vandenhoeck & Ruprecht

Bibliographic information published by the Deutsche Nationalbibliothek

The Deutsche Nationalbibliothek lists this publication in the Deutsche Nationalbibliografie; detailed bibliographic data available online: http://dnb.d-nb.de.

ISBN 978-3-525-58041-7
ISBN 978-3-647-58041-8 (E-Book)

Typesetting by SchwabScantechnik, Göttingen
Printed and bound in Germany by ⊕ Hubert & Co., Göttingen

Printed on non-aging paper.

Content

4. "But Why Are You Called a Christian?"
A Brief Commentary on the Heidelberg Catechism

Part I: Misery

Part II: Deliverance

Acknowledgements

Writing a book is never the doing of just one person, but always involves more people than just the author.

I am happy to thank Jörg Persch who suggested this project, and Silke Hartmann who guided it through the process of publication with great skill, patience, and amicability. It was indeed a pleasure working with the staff of Vandenhoeck & Ruprecht, and I am grateful for all their expert assistance. I am also very much indebted to Christopher De La Cruz, Princeton/NY, for his accurate reading and correction of the manuscript; of course I am responsible myself for all remaining errors. Most of all, I am grateful to my family – Ibrahim, Leila Marie, Alexander and Julian – for their ongoing support, understanding, and encouragement during the creation of the book, even though writing it put a strain on our family life occasionally.

This book is dedicated with deepest gratitude to two teachers, colleagues, and friends:

Eberhard Busch and Shirley C. Guthrie (†)

through whose ministry in church and academy the comfort of the Gospel has been brought to light time and again.

1. Learning By Heart.
Encountering the Heidelberg Catechism

Encounters

Even though it happened more than thirty years ago, I still vividly remember my first encounter with the Heidelberg Catechism. During our three years of weekly confirmation classes in a small-town, rather traditional Reformed congregation in Northern Germany, we had to memorize more than half of its 129 questions and answers, and, to put it mildly, we did not like it much. The questions were hard to memorize, and most of them did not, if truth be told, make any sense to us teenagers. Memorizing them was a boring duty, something you simply had to do in order to pass the confirmation exam. The Heidelberg Catechism, one of the most affectionate confessional documents not only of the Reformed, but of the entire Christian, tradition, did not touch our hearts. But that rather indifferent attitude towards the Heidelberg Catechism changed considerably when our pastor, in an attempt to bring the catechism to life, told us several stories about how people actually experienced comfort and joy through it during difficult periods of their lives, how fundamentally influential particularly the first question had been and still was to many people in the Reformed tradition, and how the catechism was for them so much more than just a schoolbook. We were surprised to learn that even people suffering from dementia regained some sort of focused consciousness for a short time while listening to parts of the Heidelberg Catechism. People on their deathbed frequently asked the pastor to pray with them either Psalm 23 or – the first question of the Heidelberg Catechism. Clearly, this text had touched *their* hearts and minds in a way we could not quite comprehend. The Heidelberg Catechism did not become our favorite book overnight, but we began to understand that it may talk to us in different ways at different times, and that it actually may have a connection to our own lives as well. We began to understand that truly encountering the Heidelberg Catechism is not about memorizing passages from an antiquated textbook for confirmation exams, but about learning with it and from it who God is for us – and who we are as those belonging to God.

This year, all over the world Reformed churches, scholars, ministers, and lay people celebrate the 450th anniversary of the Heidelberg Catechism, one of the most influential and widely used Christian books throughout the course of history and on all continents. As such, the catechism with its affectionate piety and doctrinal lucidity constitutes one of the principal testimonies of faith not only as a Reformed Confession, but as the property of the entire Protestant Reformation. For a great number of churches of the Reformed tradition, the Heidelberg Catechism is not only a vital part of their confessional heritage and doctrinal standards, but a living witness in catechesis, liturgy, preaching, devotion, and Christian living. They welcome the opportunity to not only commemorate a historical, if basically outdated document, but to listen anew to this voice from the past and learn from and with it, not only with their minds but also with their hearts. The English expression "learning by heart" could have been invented in order to describe the kind of learning the Heidelberg Catechism envisioned, where feelings and intellect are not separated, where the lessons become part of the person's living and lived knowledge, containing affective as well cognitive elements. This expression, based on the ancient Greek understanding of the heart as the seat of intelligence, memory, and emotion, captures in a rather remarkable way the purpose and aim of the Heidelberg Catechism: to engage the intellectual as well as emotional faculties of each believer in order to enable them to give an account of their faith *and* to experience the comfort of God's grace. In short, to apply the gospel message to their own lives in all dimensions, to learn Jesus Christ by heart. This understanding of faith as "sure knowledge and wholehearted trust" (question 21), which forms the basis of the whole catechism, is a gift the Heidelberg Catechism offered to its first audience and is still offering to us today. Encountering the Heidelberg Catechism today, then, invites us to share in this learning by heart.

Most contemporary Reformed Christians probably encounter the Heidelberg Catechism primarily in confirmation classes, Sunday schools or in the liturgy of worship services, though this actually varies quite a bit from church to church and congregation to congregation. The catechism was designed, though, with an even broader perspective in mind, to which we now turn.

Catechetical Textbook – Confessional Standard – Lectionary – Liturgical Element – House- and Prayerbook – Guide to Christian Living

In working through the Heidelberg Catechism and its origins, we will discover how applicable it was in different areas of church life, which may have been one of the central factors contributing to its enduring success in churches of the Reformed tradition. From the beginning, the authors of the catechism envisioned a document that would not serve only catechetical purposes in teaching children and youth but a book of Christian faith usable in different areas of church life as well as in the personal life of faith. Chapter 2 will provide us with a brief historical overlook of the origin of the Heidelberg Catechism; it might be helpful, though, to notice already here that the catechism was drafted not as a stand-alone document of Christian faith as conceived from a Reformation perspective, but as a part of a new *church order*. As such, it was placed in between the sections of the church order dealing with Baptism and the Lord's Supper, thus providing a sort of linkage, "a path of instruction" (Wim Verboom) guiding the baptized believer from his or her baptism as an infant (which was the rule in those days) towards participation in the Lord's Supper as a mature and responsible believer, entering into the communication of faith as an educated and knowledgeable believer. In order to enable and empower each believer and the Christian community as a whole to become conversant with Christian faith, its teachings as well as its practical implications for Christian life, the Heidelberg Catechism was designed with at least five purposes in mind, at which we will briefly look at below.

a) The catechetical purpose: The word catechism derives from the Greek term for teaching, originally denoting oral teaching, and thus describing more an event between teacher and pupils than a schoolbook. This aspect is kept in the question-answer-form, which is till now characteristic for catechisms. In the ancient church, catechetical teaching was used to teach the adult believers *before* their baptism, preparing them for making their confession to Christ. The most important catechetical material consistently was composed of four major parts: the Apostles' Creed, the Lord's Prayer, the Sacraments, and the Ten Commandments. When infant baptism became the rule, catechetical teaching became less important in church life for centuries, gaining importance again only at the beginning of the 16th century. The pre-Reformation movement of the Bohemian Brothers, following the reformer Jan Hus, developed its "Questions for Children" in 1502 and thereby started off a flood of new catechisms. Reformation movements all over Germany and Europe began to produce catechisms in astonishingly great numbers, reflecting the emphasis on teaching all believers the contents and implications of Christian faith as understood by the Reformation. The invention of printing and the humanist school reform made the dissemination of religious subject matters possible to an unprecedented extent. The most notable and influential catechisms from the Lutheran reformation are, without a doubt, Luther's Small and Large Catechism written in 1529, which superseded all other catechisms. The Reformed branch of the Reformation also produced a great number of catechisms with differing influence and in various regions, among them the Zurich Catechism (1534), Calvin's Genevan Catechism (1542), the Emden Catechism (1554), and as a latecomer the Smaller and Larger Westminster Catechisms (1649). In this broad field of Reformed and Reformation catechisms, the Heidelberg Catechism certainly occupies a prominent position, not least so because of its worldwide use throughout the centuries as a textbook and teaching aid within the church, but also in school and even universities and seminaries.

b) The confessional purpose: In times of doctrinal controversies, which threatened to split the church, not only in the Palatinate where the Heidelberg Catechism originated, but all over Germany and even throughout the rest of Europe, the Heidelberg Catechism was designed also as a creedal statement in the sense of a doctrinal standard to establish firm doctrinal ground for the proclamation of the gospel. As we will later see, the authors of the Heidelberg Catechism sought to define this ground as a kind of common, mediating ground between the different camps of Lutheran and Reformed churches and theologians, though without resounding success in this matter. The Heidelberg Catechism later came to be included into many church orders all over Europe, as a guide and test for doctrinally sound teaching, preaching, and church life. Its inclusion into the three so-called *Documents of Unity* by the famous Synod of Dort (1618/19) would especially lead to its confessional character in churches all over the world from the Netherlands, to South Africa, Asia, and North America.

c) The homiletical and liturgical purpose: The fourth edition of the Heidelberg Catechism from 1563 was sub-divided into 52 sections, the so-called 52 Lord's Days. With the Heidelberg Catechism, the new church order of the Palatinate developed an additional church service on Sunday afternoons called "catechism service" in which the Heidelberg Catechism served as a kind of consecutive lectionary in providing with its 52 sections the texts for the so-called "catechetical sermons" or "catechism preaching", a rather didactic form of preaching and teaching. Thus the congregation would be lead through the whole catechism once each year. Even though this practice of catechism services has lost its influence in most Reformed churches, there are churches scattered throughout that still practice this today. In addition, the Heidelberg Catechism was sub-divided into 9 sections, which would be read during Sunday morning worship services as part of the liturgy. We also still find this practice in many Reformed churches all over the world, where the Heidelberg Catechism is considered a non-negotiable liturgical element of Sunday morning worship services. This use of the Heidelberg Catechism in preaching and liturgy reflects the catechism's own style as the preaching catechism of a worshipping community.

d) The devotional purpose: Alongside this "public" use of the Heidelberg Catechism in teaching, confessing, preaching, and liturgy, the importance of it lay without a doubt also in its use for personal piety as devotional literature. Not only the last six of its questions, which are written as a prayer addressing God directly, but all of the catechism was widely used for private devotion and edification, especially as a so-called "housebook" for families. As we have said, its warm and affectionate tone endeared it to many believers, becoming a prototype for later devotional literature. As a prayer book, the Heidelberg Catechism, and in particular its first question, also played a particularly helpful role in pastoral care. From the beginning, the Heidelberg Catechism was understood as a book of comfort and consolation especially for the sick and afflicted, and already in 1563 ministers in the Palatinate were advised to read the first question at believers' sick- and deathbeds.

   e) The ethical purpose: Often times overlooked is the last of the uses of the Heidelberg Catechism, which we could describe as a "guide to Christian living", or "ethical guideline". From the beginning, the Heidelberg Catechism was understood as a guide not only for believing with your heart and mind, but with all of your life. As Frederick III, the so-called "father of the Heidelberg Catechism", remarked in his preface to the catechism, the Heidelberg Catechism was written explicitly with the aim "to promote peace, quiet and virtuous living among our subjects". Already in the first question, we find this ethical orientation of the believer's life when the Heidelberg Catechism confesses our only comfort in life and death as belonging to God "who makes me wholeheartedly willing and ready from now on to live for him". In addition, the complete third part of the catechism understands the Christian life as a life of gratitude of the believer; the catechism as a summary of faith is "relentless in its applications for our style of life in the world" (Howard Hageman). Thus the Heidelberg Catechism attempts to provide throughout a form of ethical guideline for believers, always trying to illuminate practical implications of its teachings and never separating faith and life, doctrine and praxis. The 400th anniversary edition of the Heidelberg Catechism, authorized by the North American Area Council of the World Alliance of Reformed and Presbyterian Churches, captured this intention appropriately in referring to the Heidelberg Catechism in its foreword as "a handbook of practical religion".

When we now look at a few examples of the impact of this small book, these manifold uses and applications of the Heidelberg Catechism may help explain, at least partly, its lasting and widespread success.

Small Book, Big Impact

Studying, researching, and teaching Reformed theology, in particular Reformed confessional documents, first within the German and then in an international context, I was repeatedly struck by the vitality this centuries-old text has retained for individuals as well as communities of faith within the Reformed tradition in different parts of the world. Four brief examples from Reformed churches in different contexts might help illustrate this still present influence and authority of the Heidelberg Catechism in the 20th and 21st century:

(1) One of the most important confessional documents of the 20th century is the *Theological Declaration of Barmen,* written in 1934 by the Confessing Church in Germany against the majority of Protestant churches, led by the so-called "German Christians" and aligned to the Nazi-Regime. With its first thesis following evidently the formulation of the first question of the Heidelberg Catechism, the Barmen Theological Declaration directs believers immediately to the center of the Christian faith, Jesus Christ. At the same time, the Declaration also places itself firmly and ostentatiously in the tradition of the Heidelberg Catechism, thus claiming to be the true heir of the Reformation over against the official churches. This was no coincidence or ecclesio-political move, but it came from the theological and devotional heart of this resistance movement where the Heidelberg Catechism played a central role in these congregations and for the movement's leading figures. One illuminating example of countless others is the story of Paul Schneider, a Reformed pastor and martyr. The Heidelberg Catechism proved to be an essential force for his resistance against German Christians in preaching, teaching, church discipline, and especially in his personal piety. Together with the presbytery, he had excommunicated two local Nazis from his congregation with reference to the understanding of church discipline in the Heidelberg Catechism and refused unwaveringly to give in to pressure from the Nazi regime. When he was subsequently imprisoned in 1937, he asked his wife to send him the Heidelberg Catechism to the prison so that he might study and be comforted by it. After he was martyred by the Nazis in the concentration camp of Buchenwald in 1939, he was commemorated in his funeral address by relating quotes from the

Heidelberg Catechism to certain events in his life, with question 1 at the theological heart of the commemoration.

(2) Fifty years later in a completely different context, the Heidelberg Catechism played a decisive role in yet another resistance movement and confessional development: the struggle against the theological justification of apartheid in South Africa. As part of the confessional heritage of the *Dutch Reformed Mission Church* (today forming the *Uniting Reformed Churches in Southern Africa* together with the *Dutch Reformed Church*), the Heidelberg Catechism helped facilitate a strong Reformed criticism of the apartheid system and theology in church and state. In particular, the Heidelberg Catechism's understanding of the nature of the church as a community called by God from the *entire human family* (question 54) encouraged and supported a new or rather re-newed ecclesiological vision over against the oppressive and ultimately heretical status quo in Apartheid South Africa, manifesting itself in the now famous Belhar Confession of the Dutch Reformed Mission Church from 1982. In quoting the Heidelberg Catechism directly at central junctions and thus reclaiming the Reformed heritage, the Belhar Confession confesses in Article 1 and 2, respectively: "We believe in the triune God, Father, Son and Holy Spirit, *who gathers, protects and cares for his Church by his Word and Spirit, as He has done since the beginning of the world and will do to the end.* ... We believe in one holy, universal Christian church, *the communion of saints called from the entire human family.*" Although these formulations may sound rather unspectacular in our ears, they did indeed help develop a theological (and political) courage, comfort and assertiveness, which sustained many believers in their struggles and fights for a church and state without racial separation and discrimination. This language may still have an impact on many contemporary churches in North America and other continents concerning their various own struggles with racism and discrimination; especially since a number of churches from the Reformed and Presbyterian tradition, such as the Reformed Church in America, the Christian Reformed Church in America, and the Presbyterian Church (U.S.A.) either adopted the Belhar Confession in various ways or are considering adopting it, *and* count the Heidelberg Catechism among one of their confessional standards.

(3) At roughly the same time as the Belhar Confession, the *Presbyterian Church (U.S.A.),* the new church body that came out of the union between the *Presbyterian Church in the United States* and the *United Presbyterian Church in the United States of America,* called for a new common confession that came to be named the Brief Statement of Faith (1983). The Brief Statement, representing a contemporary confession of Christian faith, including the major themes of the Reformed tradition, was deeply influenced by the theology of the Heidelberg Catechism. Not only do we find cross-references to almost all of the 129 of the Heidelberg Catechism's questions throughout the whole Statement, indicating an intimate theological relatedness to its confessional ancestor, we also encounter in its opening line, setting the tone for all that is to follow, an almost direct quotation from the Heidelberg Catechism's famous first question. The answer to this question asking about the only comfort of the believer in life and death provides us with a sort of summary of the central message of the gospel: we belong to God. That is what Christian faith is about; that is what the Heidelberg Catechism had brought up to light in the 16th century, and that is what is at the heart of Christian faith to this day. Though more than 400 years old, the Heidelberg Catechism assisted in facilitating a contemporary confession for a church that could not differ more from the church of its origins. The enduring relevance of the Heidelberg Catechism for churches in the United States stemming from the Reformed tradition is also highlighted by the recently produced new translation, which was prepared by a committee with members from *three* denominations, the *Christian Reformed Church in North America,* the *Reformed Church in America,* and the already mentioned *Presbyterian Church (U.S.A.).* As a product of intense ecumenical collaboration, this new translation of the Heidelberg Catechism is envisioned to function as a confessional bridge between three churches – a vision that would surely obtain approval from the authors of the Heidelberg Catechism.

(4) Moving to yet another continent, we find a different and rather exceptional approach in appropriating the Heidelberg Catechism for a church in the 21st century. The *Christian Church from North Central Java* (Indonesia), the *GKJTU,* founded in 1937 and originating from missionary efforts of two interdenominationally working

agencies from the Netherlands and Germany (who deliberately did not impose a confession of faith on this new church), decided in 1988 to accept the Heidelberg Catechism as its creed. With accepting this particular confession, the church defined its own identity as "Calvinist-pietistic-contextual", or simply "reformational". Unlike other Asian Reformed churches, the GJKTU did not formulate a new creed as a faithful response to contemporary and contextual challenges, but considered the Heidelberg Catechism as comprising "the basic teaching for the reformational churches throughout all the ages", "the summary of the Holy Scriptures and the basic doctrine of the GKJTU" and thus not open to revision or substitution. Yet in order to help believers facing the "many problems and struggles in their day to day life", the GKJTU adopted in 2008 a small booklet as a "Supplement to the Heidelberg Catechism", with its complete title displaying the challenging contemporary issues it addresses: "The teaching of the GKJTU on Culture, Religious Plurality and Denominational Variety, Politics, Economy as well as on Science, Arts, and Technology". Written in a simple language, it is supposed to be used – very much like the Heidelberg Catechism – not only in confirmation classes, but also in the wider context of the church's life, in preaching, liturgy, church and parish media, and Bible study groups. Modeled after the Heidelberg Catechism, the supplement applies the Question – Answer – Scriptural citations design, and uses a great number of cross-references in order to closely link these two documents of faith. Reading through this document, one is impressed by the efforts of an Indonesian church in the 21st century to appropriate its own confessional heritage in a faithful, yet contemporary and contextual way, in conversation with a document from 16th century Europe.

These four examples out of countless others might give us just a first idea of the vitality and influence of this 450-year-old textbook from a small German territory on the Upper Rhine, and the role it plays as one of the strongest ecumenical bonds of Reformed churches worldwide.

We should not overlook the fact, though, that the Heidelberg Catechism also left a trace of spiritual repression and domination, of cultural and religious imperialism in several countries, societies, and churches on which it was imposed not only as a document of faith, but also as a form of a "colonizing book" by which the "natives" were not only to be converted to Christian faith in a rather narrow confessional way, but also supposed to be "civilized". It may not come as a surprise, then, that after becoming independent, several churches actually formulated new creeds and confessions replacing those they had inherited from European churches, including the Heidelberg Catechism.

In addition, the Heidelberg Catechism has left its imprint not only on confessional documents and developments of Reformed churches worldwide, but also in the religious lives of countless individuals, and we find marks of this impact in numerous personal testimonies throughout the centuries – positive as well as negative ones. While the Heidelberg Catechism brings to light the comfort of the gospel in a "joyful, thankful, free, personal way" (Shirley Guthrie) for many, there are others who experienced it as "wooden and bloodless" (Gottfried Keller, a famous 19th century writer from Switzerland). While it enabled generations of believers to actively and responsibly participate in the communication of their faith, at times it was misused as a spiritless and restrictive instrument that turned the believers into passive recipients of a deposit of doctrinal truth, bringing about enforced doctrinal conformity, even denunciation and exclusion of those who dared to think "unorthodox" thoughts, creating a rigid defense of confessional and theological narrow-mindedness, which frequently resulted in indifference or outright rejection by many laypeople as well as theologians or pastors in Reformed churches. The Heidelberg Catechism, despite its undeniable and extraordinary success throughout centuries and all over the world, remains, just like all human writings, ambiguous in the hands of its readers and teachers. Alongside its success story, we also find stories of boredom, stuffiness, pain, and even repression inflicted by an uninspired or oppressive teaching of the Heidelberg Catechism.

The Heidelberg Catechism has also been criticized extensively, rightly or wrongly so needs to be decided in each case, for a supposedly individualistic perspective and anthropocentrism (focusing on humanity on the expense of the rest of creation), for its teaching of an angry God who demands satisfaction and chooses only a limited group for salvation, for its exclusively male language and imagery, and for a plenitude of other reasons which seem incompatible with theological and exegetical insights gained over the past centuries. At the same time, it has been praised as "a remarkably warm-hearted and personalized confession of faith, eminently deserving of its popularity among Reformed churches to the present day", as the Christian Reformed Church in North America formulates in its introduction of the Heidelberg Catechism. Of course, 21st century Christians may have and indeed should have many questions to ask this text from the 16th century, and may find some of its teachings debatable, incomprehensible, outdated, or even unbiblical. Before we can enter into a conversation with it and give voice to our criticism *or* consent, however, we should at least begin with listening to it carefully and trying to understand the catechism in its context. Consequently, this *Introduction to the Heidelberg Catechism* tries to listen carefully to this significant voice of the time of the Reformation in order to become acquainted with its teachings, but also in order to provide a starting point for a critical conversation with it. Yet this *Introduction* is also guided by an additional assumption that should be named right at the beginning: the Heidelberg Catechism is understood not only as an antique textbook, which we could read as impartial and objective readers, but as a book that constantly challenges us to ponder the age old and ever new question: "But why are you called a Christian?" As a witness to God's grace in Jesus Christ, it invites us to be drawn into the catechism's conversation of faith as partners in an ongoing dialogue on our only comfort in life and death.

The 450th anniversary of the Heidelberg Catechism provides us with an opportunity to open this book of Christian teaching once again, or maybe for the first time, encountering it not only as a historical document, but as a living testimony of faith. In maintaining with the famous Swiss theologian, Karl Barth, that the Heidelberg Catechism "deserves at least respectful hearing", this *Introduction to the Heidelberg Catechism* intends to help facilitating a first or recurrent listening to one of the milestones of Christian literature in introducing its historical background (chapter 2), its theological composition (chapter 3), as well as its main theological themes in a brief commentary on its 129 questions (chapter 4).

2. Disputes, Doctrines, and Decisions.
The Historical and Theological Background
of the Heidelberg Catechism

Like most of the major Reformation confessions of the 16th century, the Heidelberg Catechism is the result of a host of different and complex issues with theological as well as political roots. Consequently, the Heidelberg Catechism needs to be seen and understood in its specific context, if we really want to get an idea of the depth and profundity of it. For even though the catechism turned out to be one of the most enduring and inspiring texts of the Reformation throughout the centuries and around the world, it does, obviously, have a quite particular context, to which we will turn now for a brief account of its historical circumstances and of its reception throughout the following centuries.

The catechism originated in the German city of Heidelberg in 1563 in response to various doctrinal disputes with enormous political implications, involving an impressive number of academic and pastoral theologians, officials, statesmen, and other concerned parties. As a "late fruit on the tree of Reformation" (Eberhard Busch), the Heidelberg Catechism is at the same time the product of already more than 40 years of Protestant Reformation not only in Germany but all over Europe, and a bridge into the age of Protestant Orthodoxy. Concentrating on a few of the major players and disputes, we will review briefly the history of the origin of the Heidelberg Catechism with broad strokes, beginning with Frederick III, the so-called "Father of the Heidelberg Catechism", and one of the "unsung heroes" of the Reformation (John Hesselink).

Frederick, the Pious and the Palatine Reformation

Even before ascending the throne of the Palatine Electorate, a small territory located at both sides of the upper Rhine and one of the seven great principalities of the Holy Roman Empire at that time, Frederick III (1515–1576) demonstrated an extraordinary interest in theological arguments and discussions as well as a profound personal piety; he later became known as Frederick "the Pious". Born in 1515 (two years before the German monk Martin Luther nailed his 95 theses on the door of the Castle Church in Wittenberg and started what later became known as the Protestant Reformation), Frederick and his life could serve as a symbol of the religious turmoil of those days. As a descendant of the noble House of Wittelsbach, Frederick was raised and educated at the courts and universities of Nancy, Liège, and Brussels as a strict adherent to the Roman Catholic faith. At the age of 22, he married the 18-year-old princess Marie of Brandenburg-Kulmbach. Unlike many other marriages of their time, theirs seems to have been a truly happy and intimate one. Even though we do not know a great deal about Marie, she appears to have been an intelligent and gifted woman, well-known for her thorough knowledge of the Bible due to her education, which was, in contrast to her husband's, firmly based on the new Lutheran teachings. Years of theological discussion, especially with his wife Marie, and long hours of bible study convinced Frederick to leave the Roman Catholic church and to become a follower of the Reformation movement; in 1546 he publicly professed his Lutheran faith. But that profession did not end his theological studies. Much to the displeasure of his wife, who remained an ardent Lutheran to her death ("I have learned one [the Lutheran] catechism, and I will adhere to it!"), Frederick became interested in the theology of the Reformed branch of the Protestant Reformation, which was inaugurated mainly by Swiss and French reformers such as Zwingli, Bucer, Bullinger, and especially by John Calvin in Geneva. All over Germany, however, theologians of the different branches of the Reformation were in serious dispute with each other over theological doctrines, spending a vast amount of time and energy in repudiating dissenting opinions, even condemning the other side as heretical. The Reformation had clearly entered a crucial stage: the hard-won doctrinal truths of this renewal movement had to be established, the danger of a sectarian splintering of the Reformation had to be averted, and, most important of all, the laypeople had to be taught how to live the Protestant faith.

When Frederick III ascended to the throne in Heidelberg in 1559, he found there complicated and difficult circumstances fraught with all sorts of theological controversies and tensions going back to the early 1520s. At that time, Reformation ideas had entered the Electoral Palatinate, in sermons as well as in academic lectures, and had started a sort of popular Reformation movement "from below", initially without official support from the authorities. Due to the rather erratic course of sometimes tolerating Lutheran reforms in his land, sometimes defending Roman Catholic positions, Frederick's pre-predecessor (Frederick II) had created the odd and very unstable situation of one land undecided between two confessions for more than two decades. Only in 1546, the Lutheran Reformation was legally introduced into the Palatinate by the authorities, consenting with an apparent public desire for reformation. No more than two years later, though, all Protestant territories were forced, by the imperial order of Charles V, to return to the Roman Catholic order. The Palatinate did not constitute an exception: the Reformation was officially revoked, even though no real changes in the staffing of influential administrative and ecclesial positions occurred. Protestant Reformation went, in a manner of speaking, dormant for almost a decade in Heidelberg, until the so-called Religious Peace of Augsburg in 1555 was established, which officially brought the religious conflicts between Roman Catholicism and Lutheranism to an end, giving all states' princes of the Holy Roman Empire permission to choose for them and their domain either Catholicism or Lutheranism as the official religion. The legal status of Reformed territories, though, remained vague and precarious, since the Peace of Augsburg explicitly applied only to those Protestant territories adhering to the Lutheran Augsburg Confession. Frederick's formally Lutheran-minded predecessor, Otto Henry (who also was privately in contact with Bullinger, Zwingli's successor in Zurich!), had subsequently reintroduced the Lutheran confession in 1556, and called a rather diverse group of prominent Protestant scholars (strict and mild Lutherans, Calvinists and Zwinglians) to the faculties of the renowned and almost 500-year-old University of Heidelberg. Reflecting the virulent inner-Protestant tensions at the time, these scholars almost immediately started to quarrel with each other over theological issues, arising especially out of the much-discussed issue of the Lord's Supper. Consequently, the pulpits of the University of

Heidelberg and of its many churches turned into the battleground of some sort of "pulpit war" over the correct understanding of the modality of Christ's presence in the Eucharist. In addition, since the Reformation had not been implemented thoroughly in all regions of the Palatinate, the population was confused and upset, the parishes lacking qualified guidance by educated ministers. In short, the state of affairs in Heidelberg and the Palatinate was a mess in many respects and desperately needed to be straightened up in order to restore public peace in church and state.

Doctrinal Disputes over the Lord's Supper

Before continuing with the progress of events in Heidelberg, we need to pause for a moment in order to give some attention to the theological discussions at hand: What exactly were those opposing Protestant camps in Heidelberg, the Palatinate, all over Germany, and in many other parts of Europe fighting about? What confessional controversies led them to wage a doctrinal war against each other to the extent that they were actually endangering all that had been accomplished by the Reformation movement before? As mentioned earlier, at the center of these disputes stood differing views on Christ's presence in the Eucharist, constituting the key point of difference between Reformed and Lutheran theologies not only for the 16th century, but for centuries to come. The central question turned out to be how to understand Christ's words "This is my body" [Mt 26:26] at the Last Supper, or, to be more specific, how the signs (bread and wine) are related to what is signified (Christ's Body and Blood/forgiveness of sins). A brief, and thus necessarily oversimplifying, outline of the different positions on that issue may be useful:

– The Roman Catholic Church interpreted those words of Christ quite literally: even though the communicants still see and taste bread and wine in the Eucharist, the substance of it actually has been transformed into the substance of Christ's Body and Blood; the communicants truly receive Christ's Body and Blood. The signs have been changed or transubstantiated into the things signified; this understanding is accordingly known as the doctrine of "transubstantiation".

- The Lutheran understanding, on the other hand, claimed that the substance of bread and wine does not change at all. The substance of Christ's Body and Blood, however, is really present, and the communicants receive them "in, with, and under" the elements of bread and wine, thus asserting a *sacramental union* (Luther) of the signs with the things signified. It is only through this sacramental union that believers receive salvation and forgiveness of sin. This doctrine is also known as "consubstantiation".

- A somewhat different, but for the Heidelberg Catechism critical position, is that of Phillip Melanchthon, Luther's collaborator, the intellectual leader of the Lutheran reformation and, at a later time, a theological counselor of Frederick III. Melanchthon had changed his position from a form of consubstantiation (in the Augsburg Confession in 1530) to a more intermediate position (in the 1540 altered edition of the Augsburg Confession), which was more agreeable to Reformed theologians by emphasizing that bread and wine are real signs of Christ's presence, which is located in the use of the meal or action of distributing the bread rather than in the element itself.

- Reformed theologians, now, did agree with all Lutherans in rejecting the Roman Catholic doctrine of transubstantiation, but did not accept the stricter Lutheran understanding of Christ's real presence "in, with, and under" the elements. To make things even more complicated, Reformed theologians advocated rather different conceptions of the issue at hand; the main thinkers followed Zwingli and Calvin:

  • The followers of Huldrych Zwingli, reformer of Zurich, supported a more symbolic view of the Eucharist: the elements of bread and wine only point the communicants to Christ's Body and Blood, signifying them without literally turning into them. Signs and things signified are strictly separated, because the Risen Christ in his humanity (and consequently his body and blood), is not to be found on earth in any kind of element, but is seated at the right hand of his Father in Heaven. Therefore, the communicants do not receive Christ's Body and Blood. The Last Supper is an act of thanksgiving for God's gift of grace. Zwingli had based this view on Lk 22:19 ("Do this in remembrance of me"), but it would be misleading to reduce his understanding to a form of bare symbolic memorialism, as it is often done, since the Zwinglians did indeed "believe Christ to be truly present in the Supper" (Zwingli), only in no way bound to the elements of bread and wine, but in the form of a spiritual rather than physical presence. This essential difference of opinion had caused Luther to exclaim at the end of the famous Marburg Colloquy (which was convened in order to dissolve the dispute over the Real Presence in 1529) to one of Zwingli's associates: "You have a different spirit than ours!" – a statement describing the rift within the Reformation movement that was not to be closed until more than 400 years later.

- The followers of John Calvin, reformer of Geneva, though, found themselves actually, and maybe for some surprisingly so, closer to Luther than to Zwingli in emphasizing Christ's genuine union with us through the Lord's Supper through which we receive God's gift of grace. With Zwingli, Calvin would describe the elements as signs pointing to Christ, separated from the things signified: bread and wine do not turn into Christ's Body and Blood, communicants do not receive them "in, with, and under" the elements, because Christ's body is located in a certain place in heaven. But with Luther, Calvin would fervently argue for a sacramental (though mystical) union of Christ with the believers by faith: through the work of the Holy Spirit in the sacramental act, the believer is spiritually united with the Risen and Ascended Christ with the elements being visible instruments of an invisible reality. Through the Lord's Supper, Christ is indeed communicating Himself and God's gifts of grace (the thing signified) to the believers by means of bread and wine (the signs). The Calvinist understanding, therefore, could be described as a "symbolic instrumentalism".

It may seem like a purely academic, and maybe even obsolete, theological discussion to 21st century Christians, yet for 16th century believers this discussion dealt with the core of their faith: how are we united to Christ and receive God's gift of grace, the forgiveness of our sins? In these angst-ridden times, in the midst of religious as well as political turmoil, people deeply cared about this question. To them it appeared to be decisive for their eternal salvation, and erring in it may condemn them to damnation. In addition, it did not constitute a merely theological question, but actually a highly political subject with dramatic potential effects: for a sovereign to choose (for himself and thus also for his people) any of these opinions had immediate legal consequences. Either he was covered by the Peace of Augsburg (Catholics and Lutherans) and thus protected by the Holy Roman Empire, or he faced immediate repudiation by the Emperor, losing his territories or maybe even his life.

Controversy and Conciliation in Heidelberg

It goes without saying that there was no way to be indifferent about this issue, especially not if you were the sovereign, as Frederick III was, of one of the leading principalities of the Empire, if your subjects were at serious odds with each other over this controversy, and if you yourself had a vested interest in bringing about appeasement on a sound theological basis. The situation in the Electoral Palatinate in the middle of the 16th century could, thus, rightly be described as being all about *controversy and conciliation* (Derk Visser); and when Frederick took over government affairs, he immediately set out to clear up the confusion and to mediate the conflicts in order to bring about conciliation and unification. Even though the Heidelberg Catechism is known as one of the most important and influential texts of the *Reformed* tradition, it quite obviously breathes this spirit of conciliation, attempting to steer a sort of middle course between the opposing camps, while trying to remain uncompromisingly faithful to the rediscovered Biblical truths of the Reformation. In contrast to many of his royal contemporaries, Frederick himself never took to thinking in theological or ecclesio-political stereotypes; on the contrary, in a letter to three of his royal colleagues in 1563 he wrote, in defense of the Heidelberg Catechism, that he himself praised God for "being a Christian, baptized in the name of Christ, and not in the name of Zwingli, Calvin, Luther, or however they are named".

Against this theological background, we return now to the course of events in Heidelberg. On the eve of the death of Frederick's predecessor in 1559, Otto Henry, the conflict in the church of the Palatinate and the University of Heidelberg had escalated into a bitter controversy over the Lord's Supper between the Lutheran church superintendent and theology professor, Heshusius, and the rather Zwinglian deacon of Heidelberg, Klebitz. Their doctrinal warfare soon spread out all over university, church, and town, until the new Elector Palatinate himself intervened. When all attempts to mediate between them failed spectacularly (with the deliberately provoked Klebitz resorting to actual physical violence!), Frederick dismissed both of the adversaries. That did not close the matter for him, however. Quite the contrary, Frederick decided to get to the bottom of things and find a conclusive theological understanding of Christ's presence in the Lord's Supper based on the Bible. After intensive theological studies and even requesting a theological assessment of the issues at hand from Melanchton (which turned out to lean more towards the Reformed interpretation of the Lord's Supper than to the stricter Lutheran interpretation), Frederick used the occasion of his daughter's wedding to a Saxon prince in 1560 for what would later be called the "Heidelberg Lord's Supper Disputation" or the "Wedding Debates" between the Saxon (Lutheran) and Palatinate (Reformed) theologians. In the course of the debate, the previously undecided Frederick was won over to the Reformed side by, as he stated, the simplicity of the arguments particularly of Thomas Erastus, professor of medicine, principal of the Heidelberg University, and the personal physician of the elector. And yet, Frederick was still hesitant to definitively change sides from the Lutheran to the Reformed camp. Under the above mentioned Augsburg Settlement this would mean risking not only his electoral privileges, but also his territory – and, as we have said, maybe even his life. For that reason, it does not come as a surprise to see Frederick campaigning for some sort of middle course when all Protestant princes of Germany met at the Convention of Naumburg in 1561 in order to strengthen their common cause. Many, if not most, of the princes were arguing for a hard-line Lutheranism based on the Augsburg Confession of 1530, the original confession known as the *Invariata* (the "unaltered"), which did exclude Reformed convictions of the Lord's Supper and would thus also exclude Reformed territories from the protection of the Peace of Augsburg. Frederick, though, argued for the altered Augsburg Confession of 1540, the *Variata,* which was not only more tolerable for Reformed ears, but would also keep Reformed territories under the protection of the Peace of Augsburg. The princes decided in favor of the Invariata, but conceded to permit the Variata as an acceptable version and thus opening the door for a (cautiously) Reformed interpretation of the Lord's Supper. Moreover, this success paved the way for Frederick's further efforts to strengthen the Reformed reformation of the Palatinate, thus eventually leading to the creation of the Heidelberg Catechism.

Frederick proceeded with his project: he continued studying the Bible as well as theological writings, and even began a correspondence with Bullinger in Zurich, who ardently supported the Reformed reformation in the Palatinate with theological and ecclesio-political counsel. Frederick dismissed several strict Lutheran pastors and other officials (with some of them leaving by their own choice) who would not agree to a more moderate understanding of the Lord's Supper, and he opened the doors for Reformed councilors, ministers, and also faculty members. As a result, the Reformed camp in the church council, in the faculties of the university, and the Elector's cabinet gained in influence, eventually forming the majority. Particularly in university recruitment the new direction became obvious; open positions were effectively filled with scholars demonstrating Reformed convictions. Only the faculty of Divinity posed a bit of a problem; for almost two decades this faculty had unsuccessfully tried to find a renowned theologian with German as his native language in order to form and represent the particular theology of the Palatinate. The solution to this problem came in the guise of the young and remarkably gifted theologian, Zacharias Ursinus, who joined the faculty of theology in 1561, and to whom we will turn now for a short biographical sketch.

Zacharias Ursinus, the Reluctant Reformer

Ursinus, the son of a Lutheran deacon of rather modest means, was born 1534 in the Silesian city of Breslau (now Poland, then part of Austria), and it became quickly apparent that he was a brilliant and very capable student. At the age of 16, he enrolled at the Wittenberg University, where Melanchthon realized his talent and became a life-long mentor, theological ally, and close friend to him. When Ursinus proved himself to be a supreme theologian in the years that followed, Melanchthon took him along to the Colloquy of Worms in 1557, a disputation between Protestant and Roman Catholic theologians convened by the German King Ferdinand I, after which Ursinus set out for a yearlong study trip throughout Europe. On Melanch-thon's recommendation, he studied at the renowned universities of Heidelberg, Strasbourg, Basel, Geneva, and Paris, and became acquainted with the most famous theologians of his time, includ-ing the Reformed scholars and reformers Theodor Beza, Heinrich Bullinger, Petrus Martyr Vermigli and John Calvin (who even pre-sented him with a complete and signed edition of his own works). A few years after returning to his native city of Breslau, a hard-line Lutheran place, Ursinus was accused of Reformed leanings because of his support of Melanchthon's understanding of the Lord's Supper. In order to avoid ongoing bitter controversies and personal hassle, which he fervently abhorred, he resigned and moved to Zurich to work and study with the Italian reformer Petrus Martyr Vermigli, with whom he had formed a cordial friendship and who had become a leading scholar on the Reformed doctrine of the Lord's Supper. Ursinus enjoyed his peaceful sojourn with kindred spirits in Zurich, and when Vermigli declined Frederick's invitation to come to Heidel-berg and recommended Ursinus for this position in his stead, he was more than reluctant to accept the offer. He knew quite well what sort of controversies and doctrinal wars were awaiting him in Heidelberg and the Palatinate, and to him, as a rather shy and reserved person, this place did not present alluring prospects at all. He accepted the call to Heidelberg nevertheless, became the director of the newly established theological academy for training ministers in 1561, and immediately upon receiving his theological doctorate in 1562 was appointed professor of dogmatics. In the same year, Ursinus prepared two catechisms, a smaller one for teaching children and a larger one as a guide for theological instruction; both catechisms were worked into the Heidelberg Catechism later. Soon after that, Frederick sought to employ the exceptional theological scholarship of his young professor (he had turned only 28 that year!), and commissioned him together with a group of other theologians to compose a catechism, which would, in combination with a new church order and liturgy, hopefully bring all the confessional controversies in his territory to an end. Thus Ursinus became the "Reluctant Reformer" (Derk Visser), whose principal work, the Heidelberg Catechism, would turn out to be one of the most widespread and influential Christian writings of all time, and Ursinus as its main interpreter and theological apologist for decades, even centuries to come.

The Writing of the Heidelberg Catechism

Frederick had finally decided on having a new catechism for the Palatinate drawn up, which did not really come as a big surprise to anybody involved, especially since this was general practice at that time. As we have seen in Chapter One, catechisms had been around for quite some time, with the "Questions for Children" of the Bohemian Brothers (1502, published in German in 1522) breaking the ground. Soon after the Reformation movement got under way, catechisms turned up all over Europe, literally numbering in the hundreds. When Frederick was contemplating a new catechism for the Palatinate, he thus had quite a number of catechisms to refer to, several of them (Lutheran *and* Reformed!) actually in use in his own territory. Nonetheless, he decided that a new catechism was needed in order "to promote peace, quiet and virtuous living among our subjects, but also (and above all) to admonish and lead them to devout knowledge and fear of the Almighty and his holy word of salvation, as the only foundation of all virtue and obedience". [All quotations in this paragraph are taken from Frederick's own preface to the first edition of the Heidelberg Catechism.] He judged the situation in the church to be a very complicated one with "an important defect in our system" that was "exposed by the fact that young people … tend to be lax in their Christian doctrine". Having recognized the elimination of this defect as "a high obligation and most important duty of our government", Frederick aspired to have a catechism composed that would function not only as the basis for young people's catechetical instruction, but also as "a clear and fixed form and standard to follow" for pastors and schoolmasters. As we have already noted in the first chapter, the Heidelberg Catechism was designed with multiple intentions in mind: as a guide for sound teaching and preaching (the catechetical and homiletical function) as well as a consensus formula for confessional unity (the doctrinal function), as a guide to virtuous living (the ethical function), for use in worship services such as in readings before the sermon (the liturgical function), and as a book of religious edification at home (the devotional function). In order to achieve those purposes, Frederick "secured the composition of a summary course of instruction or catechism", "with the advice and cooperation of our entire theological faculty in this place, and of all superintendents and distinguished servants of the church".

Due to the fact that we have no records of the actual process of the preparation of the Heidelberg Catechism, we cannot be really sure of the historical accuracy of this last remark. Current academic research, though, seems to support the claim that the Heidelberg Catechism is indeed the result of the team work of a number of academic, pastoral, as well as proficient lay theologians – including Frederick himself, who not only commented on the draft frequently, but changed it in several places and even added a question on the Lord's Supper (question 80) after the publication of the first edition. He also insisted on adding biblical references to the text in order to proof the scripturality of this new catechism, and, more importantly, to demonstrate that all 129 questions of the catechism actually seek to be nothing else but an exposition of the biblical witness. One particular characteristic of the Heidelberg Catechism can be, therefore, traced back directly to Frederick's influence: the use of biblical references not only from the New but also from the Old Testament (which in itself was a rarity for a catechism) with the understanding that those biblical references as such were not merely "nice to have" though essentially negligible footnotes, but in fact an indispensable part of the confession. It was Frederick's as well as the other authors' intention that teaching the Heidelberg Catechism may not replace Bible study, but that instead it would stimulate and motivate believers, by themselves and as a congregation, to study the Bible as reflective, educated and accountable Christians – thereby, through the work of the Holy Spirit, meeting God, who revealed Godself in the Word.

The major and central figure in preparing the catechism was presumably the young professor of dogmatics, Zacharias Ursinus. Although we have no historical documents to conclusively prove his authorship (nowhere, probably deliberately so, is a single author identified by the sources), a consensus among contemporary scholars has developed based on growing evidence pointing towards the ire-nic-minded and extraordinarily talented Ursinus as the main drafter of the Heidelberg Catechism, with his broad theological perspective obtained during his studies with major figures of the Reformation. Working alongside him was the equally young court chaplain, pastor of Heidelberg's main Protestant church, member of the church council, and former professor of dogmatics, Caspar Olevianus, whose actual influence on the Heidelberg Catechism, though, remains disputed among scholars and may never be resolved. What we know, how-ever, is that Ursinus' shorter and longer catechism were worked into one catechism by the afore-mentioned team, the electoral council of theologians, pastor, and church superintendents convened in late fall that year by Frederick. Several other Reformed catechisms had been consulted in preparation for the new one; most prominent among them the Calvin's Genevan Catechism (which Ursinus was translating into German around that time), but also Reformed catechisms from Zurich, Emden, London, and other places – the actual number of reference catechisms varying slightly from scholar to scholar.

The Success Story of the Heidelberg Catechism

After its introduction in January 1563, the Heidelberg Catechism was an immediate and resounding success within the Palatinate where it replaced all other catechisms and was met with approval from all sides – initially anyway. The famous Reformed theologian and Swiss reformer Heinrich Bullinger was so enthusiastic about it that he even called the Heidelberg Catechism the "best catechism ever published". The catechism went through four German and one official Latin edition in the first year alone, and spread quickly all over Europe. Over the next one hundred years, German editions were printed not only in Heidelberg, but in other German cities, as well as in Amsterdam and Basel; the Latin version was printed in

places such as Antwerp, Leiden, Oxford and Edinburgh. That was
not all: early on a need and demand for translations became evident,
and already in 1563 a Dutch version (one of at least 22 Dutch ver-
sions until 1600) appeared, soon to be followed by French, English,
Scottish, Hebrew, Greek, Hungarian, Czech, Romanian, and even
Romansch translations with each of them going through different
editions. Dutch colonialism then took the Heidelberg Catechism
beyond Europe; with the East and West India Companies the catechism traveled around the globe, and was translated into Malay,
Javanese, Spanish, Portuguese, Singhalese, and Tamil in the 17th
and 18th century. In 1609, Dutch explorers brought the Heidelberg
Catechism to Manhattan Island, making it "the first Protestant confession planted on American soil" (Phillip Schaff); its importance
remaining especially in Dutch and German Reformed churches in
Pennsylvania and all over the country. Missionaries of the Dutch
Reformed Church in America added translations in Amharic, San-
giri, Arabic, Persian (Farsi), Chinese, and Japanese in the 19th century.
Another quote of Phillipp Schaff sums up this linguistic wealth quite
adequately: the Heidelberg Catechism "has the Pentecostal gift of
tongues in a rare degree."

   The significance and value of the Heidelberg Catechism for the
Reformed Community all over the world is underscored by the fact
that it quickly became part of church orders of several Reformed
churches all over Europe: the Palatinate included the Heidelberg
Catechism into its new church order in 1563, and soon after that
several German and Dutch Reformed churches approved it for use
in teaching and preaching, sometimes requiring office-bearers in
the church to subscribe to it. Already in 1567, the Synod of Debrecen
accepted the Heidelberg Catechism (in its Hungarian translation) as
its textbook for catechesis in the Reformed Church in Hungary. Over
the next years, it was also adopted in Reformed churches in Poland,
Transylvania, and, hesitantly, in Switzerland. In particular the great
Synod of Dort in 1618/-19 had a lasting impact in deciding to not only
approve the Heidelberg Catechism, but to adopt it together with the
Belgic Confessions and the Canons of Dort as one of the so-called
"Three Forms of Unity". With this decision, it provided a doctrinal
consensus for many Reformed Churches, especially those with Dutch

roots, all over the world to this day. The Heidelberg had become a symbol of and a means to Reformed identity and unity.

With this success story in mind, we do not think it is presumptuous to assume that the Heidelberg Catechism would indeed find a prominent place on an imaginary "All-Time Bestseller (and also Best-Loved) List" of Christian texts. Add to this the fact that there is a whole library of books with commentaries, interpretations, paraphrases, sermons, syllabi, critiques, and apologies all dealing with the Heidelberg Catechism in a host of languages, and the term "monumental" with which the Heidelberg Catechism is frequently labeled does actually seem appropriate.

Under Attack

Of course, however, despite this huge success (or maybe because of it?), and despite its irenic intention, the Heidelberg Catechism met with fierce opposition as well. It was attacked and condemned not only by Roman Catholic princes and bishops, but even more so by strict Lutherans, theologians as well as princes, for its alleged Zwinglian and Calvinistic tendencies and its "seditious spirit". And so the unavoidable happened: although Frederick III claimed that the catechism stood within the theological boundary drawn by the (altered) Augsburg Confession, he was charged with apostasy from the true Lutheran faith according to the Peace of Augsburg, which meant, as we said before, that he was in grave danger of losing his electoral rights, his territory, and even his life. Fearing that the bitter altercations might lead into a civil war, the rather temperate Emperor Maximilian II, who had warned Frederick before that his catechism did not agree with the Augsburg Confession, wanted this matter to be cleared up and ordered Frederick to appear at the Diet of Augsburg in 1566. Frederick was charged with "innovations" (meaning: heresy) and required to renounce his Reformed faith; his case, as well as the case of Reformed churches in Germany, seemed to be hopeless. Despite all that, Frederick remained assured and confident; defending the catechism primarily by pointing to the biblical roots of its text, claiming that "in matters of faith and conscience", he acknowledged only God as the "one Lord who is Lord of all lords, and King of all kings". Frederick's calm but steadfast petition impressed, rather unpredictably so, some of the more moderate Lutheran princes who rose to his support, with one of them, the Elector of Saxony, exclaiming after his magnificent address: "Fritz, you are more pious than all of us!" Eventually, the Emperor was also won over, and for a number of reasons (most of them actually related to political concerns), Maximilian did accept Frederick's petition, and in doing so, he *de facto* tolerated the Reformed faith as a third religion in his empire, even though it would take 72 more years for Reformed churches to receive equal rights *de jure* through the so-called Peace of Westphalia. Frederick, the "Father of Heidelberg Catechism", had become a "Protector of the Reformed Church".

Postscript: Mediation Failed

In order to be historically accurate, though, a brief postscript on the dramatic *failure* of the Heidelberg Catechism in its own context of origin is necessary at this point. In spite of its initial success in the Palatinate, the Heidelberg Catechism did not really bring together the Lutheran and Reformed camps either in the Palatinate nor, as we have seen, in Germany; it did not bring about the conciliation Frederick had longed for so fervently. Theological conflicts and adversaries even began to permeate his own family with bitter controversies between two of his sons: the elder one, Louis VI, probably influenced by his mother Marie, promoted Lutheranism, while the younger one and his father's favorite, John Casimir, leaned towards the Reformed side. When Louis came to the throne in 1576 after the death of his father, he did not abide to his father's testamentary will to maintain a Reformed orientation of the Palatinate, but revoked his father's decision in this matter, expelled all Reformed theologians including Ursinus (who like others, found refuge in John Casimir's small territory of the principality of Pfalz Lautern), and replaced all Reformed ministers by Lutherans. Upon the death of Louis in 1583, though, his 9-year old son, Frederick IV, under the guardianship of his uncle Johan Casimir, redirected the course of the Palatinate again by establishing a form of bi-confessional status (Lutheran and Reformed) of the Palatinate for some time, before returning to the Reformed church order of Frederick III in 1585 and replacing the Lutheran theologians of the Heidelberg University again with Reformed scholars. The 17th century would bring the catastrophe of the Thirty-Years' War with its devastations, confessional turmoil, and attempts of recatholization all over Germany as well as in the Palatinate. In 1705, a Declaration on Religions established three accepted religions: Reformed, Lutheran, and Roman Catholic; confessional disputes and changes, though, remained the order of the day until the Palatinate became part of the Protestant Grand Duchy of Baden in 1806. Retrospectively, one could therefore summarize the historical results of Frederick's fervent efforts for unification, mediation, and religious peace with the rather disillusioning characterization of "mediation failed" (Michael Weinrich).

3. The State We Are In.
The Theological Composition of the Heidelberg Catechism, Its Triple Knowledge and the Human Condition

The Heidelberg Catechism is no "Christian-Doctrine-Wiki", and even though it was used as a Christian textbook within Reformed churches for centuries, it is not simply a systematic discussion of major doctrines from a Reformed perspective. You may, of course, turn to its 129 questions in order to look up the Heidelberg Catechism's understanding of, let's say, infant baptism, or the Ten Commandments, or sanctification, or whatever doctrinal question you are interested in at the moment, and you will get a brief and concise answer. But that is not how the Heidelberg Catechism is supposed to be read, studied, understood, and confessed, for two reasons:

1. Unlike numerous other catechisms, the Heidelberg Catechism does not simply string together explanations of basic catechetical elements (essentially the Ten Commandments, the Apostles' Creed, the Lord's Prayer, and the Sacraments) as do other Protestant catechisms. Its theological composition, the way the Heidelberg Catechism is arranged, its outline even, is a confession in itself. Reading the headings and sub-headings will already provide us with its main theological framework within which each of its answers is to be understood and interpreted. For that reason, the Heidelberg Catechism has been called an "analytical" catechism, because it – apparently – works backwards from the outcome/effects (our comfort) to what came first (God's activity in Jesus Christ). We will get to this so-called analytical framework in more detail shortly.

2. The Heidelberg Catechism does not use some kind of neutral or abstract doctrinal language, as do, for example, the Westminster Catechisms from 1647, but it addresses the reader directly as the one who needs comfort or exhortation, who benefits from God's work in Christ, who prays with the words of the Lord; who is, in other words, directly involved in and affected by all the catechism has to say about who God is and what God does, and who we humans are as those who belong to God. Christian faith is

not understood here exclusively as a set of religious beliefs and practices you have to accept intellectually, but also as trust in and personal response to God's faithfulness. Faith is not understood "objectively" in the Heidelberg Catechism, as if it were an object that could be examined apart from the believer and the One we believe in. The Heidelberg Catechism wants to draw believers into the process and performance of believing, mediating experiences of faith, enabling the believers to account for their faith, to reflect on it communally and individually, and to be assured of the truth of the Gospel-faith given by God. Listening to the difference in tone of the first questions of the Westminster Catechism and the Heidelberg Catechism, respectively, it becomes obvious that the HC emphasizes the relation of theological doctrine and troubled believer:

Westminster Catechism: "What is the chief and highest end of *man?*"

Heidelberg Catechism: "What is *your* only comfort in life and in death?"

As we have seen before, and as we will continue to see in later chapters, the Heidelberg Catechism indeed aims at *learning by heart,* which includes both, theological correctness as well as personal involvement.

Let us turn now to the theological composition of the HC, which was agreed upon early in the drafting process, and which has become so characteristic of it throughout the centuries and all over the world. It could even be argued that the plan and method with which the Heidelberg Catechism organizes the catechetical material are one major reason for its vitality and lasting relevance (Willem van't Spijker).

"The Strange Logic of Grace"

The Heidelberg Catechism was written not only for the purpose of teaching, but was also the product of the remarkably pedagogical and didactical knowledge and experience of its authors. We encounter the prime example of this knowledge and experience in teaching, paired with an extraordinary concise theological *and* pastoral message, already in the famous and beloved first question, which has even been called "a climax of the confessional literature of all Christian ages" (Hendrikus Berkhoff):

> Q 1: What is your only comfort in life and in death?
> A. That I am not my own, but belong – body and soul – to my faithful Savior Jesus Christ. He has fully paid for all my sins with his precious blood, and has set me free from the tyranny of the devil. He also watches over me in such a way that not a hair can fall from my head without the will of my Father in heaven; in fact, all things must work together for my salvation. Because I belong to him, Christ, by his Holy Spirit, assures me of eternal life and makes me wholeheartedly willing and ready from now on to live for him.

The next chapter will discuss this question in greater detail; for now we are only interested in its core message: We belong to God, in life and death, and nothing can separate us from the love of God! And equally important: because Jesus Christ is *our* faithful Savior, because the almighty God is *our* Father in heaven, and the Holy Spirit is given to *us,* we can also confess, believe and trust in the promise that not only do we belong to God, but God, by God's own choice, does indeed belong to us. "You are mine and I am yours!" The Heidelberg Catechism repeats at this point a central rediscovery and claim of the Protestant Reformation: the assurance of salvation, that is to say, the doctrine teaching that Christian believers' can be confident of being eternally saved in Christ, solely by virtue of God's saving grace.

Accordingly, for Ursinus, author and main interpreter of the Heidelberg Catechism in his time and age, this first question did not constitute an arbitrarily chosen opening statement of the catechism with several other possible alternatives. On the contrary, according to his own commentary, he understood the first question as containing the "sum and scope of the whole catechism", and with that, the sum and scope of the Gospel – the "whole truth in a nutshell" as another commentary puts it (Andrew Kuyvenhoven). For the authors of the Heidelberg Catechism and for countless generations of Reformed Christians after them, this first question recapitulates in a unique way the comfort believers know, believe, and trust in. All that follows is only unfolding this core message of the salvific relationship between

God and human beings. The Good News of Jesus Christ, our ultimate comfort, summarized in a little more than one hundred words!

The Triple Knowledge

But, of course, this summary needs unfolding, and this is precisely
what question 2 aims at, yet again combining in a remarkable way
didactical purposes with theological substantiation:

> Q 2: What must you know to live and die in the joy of this comfort?
> A. Three things: First, how great my sin and misery are; second,
> how I am set free from all my sins and misery; third, how I am to
> thank God for such deliverance.

The catechism is still concerned with our comfort, or to be exact, with
what we need to know in order to appropriate the *joy of this comfort.*
Accommodatingly, the authors of the Heidelberg Catechism provide
us by means of this triad of knowledge not only with a fundamental
theological *insight,* with what has been called "an ingenious restatement of the essence of the whole Reformation" (Karl Barth), but also
with a clear and succinct synopsis of the *structure* of the catechism.
This triad has been termed "triple knowledge", the knowledge of
our *misery, deliverance,* and *gratitude;* at the same time, these terms
caption the three main parts of the catechism.

> First Part (q. 3–11):   Misery
> Second Part (q. 12–85):   Deliverance
> Third Part (q. 86–129):   Gratitude

Even though there is no reference to it in this place, Paul's epis-
tle to the Romans was clearly on the mind of the authors, especially Rom 7:24–25, where we do not only find the aforementioned
triad, but also the same focusing on the "I" and "me" of the believer
("Wretched man that I am! Who will rescue me from this body of
death? Thanks be to God through Jesus Christ our Lord!")[1]. Whether

---

1   For quotations from the Bible I use the New Revised Standard Version.

this three-fold structure as the main composition principle of the catechism can be traced back directly to other Reformation theologians, for instance Luther, Melanchton, Theodor Beza (Calvin's successor in Geneva), or other Lutheran, Reformed, even pre-Reformation sources, is still disputed controversially among scholars. Unambiguous and undeniable, though, is the fact that this triad quickly became a genuine and efficacious characteristic of the Heidelberg Catechism in subsequent years, and is now inseparably associated with it.

Before discussing this three-fold structure in more detail, we need to pause here for a moment in order to not completely misinterpret the catechism's intention right from the beginning. This triple knowledge dealing with the three-fold human situation is by no means a description for any form of psychological, intellectual or emotional human development, and that is crucial to understand and keep in mind. It is not our 3-step-guide to complete joy and comfort; it does not describe a chronological sequence of human conditions like a one-way road from "from rebellion to redemption", as one book on the Heidelberg Catechism is titled somewhat ambiguously. Question 2 does not talk about three different human states, but about the *one human state as a Christian* determined by three aspects simultaneously. It does not describe how we become a Christian, but analyses what it means to be a Christian. In addition, the triple knowledge is not to be understood from an exclusively anthropological (that is, human-centered) perspective; it can only be understood from the perspective of *God's prevenient grace* as the basic act and foundation of all knowledge and confession. In other words: Question 2 can only be understood adequately on the basis of Question 1. Only after confessing that we belong – in life and death – *not* to ourselves, but to our faithful and saving God, the good God of Grace, can we begin exploring our sin and misery as being alienated from God, our deliverance as being brought back into right relationship with God, and our grateful life as being enabled to live the "good life". The Heidelberg Catechism does not use the logic of a "poisonous" pedagogy (devalorizing the believer as sinful, worthless sinner) in order to make God and God's gracious acts all the greater under the premise that maximizing human sin means maximizing

God's grace. It also does not follow the logic of good works: after recognizing and confessing your sin, and doing good works you will be forgiven by God. Instead, from beginning to end, the Heidelberg Catechism follows what has been called the "strange logic of grace" (Douglas Ottati). This logic of grace, running against many, if not most, of our common assumptions, means that our eternal and unchangeable belonging to the good God of Grace is the foundation of all we believe and know about God and ourselves – a major theme in Calvin's theology as well – and that the triple knowledge only unfolds and develops in greater detail what this foundation of belonging means for us. As we have seen before: the triple knowledge tries to convey the Good News of the Gospel. Consequently, even though the first question does indeed provide the text with a warm, personal, and affective note right at the beginning, the Heidelberg Catechism is much profounder than that, not remaining at some form of spiritual "feel good" surface, but binding together our ultimate comfort with the knowledge of *God's* prevenient grace.

With the words of German theologian Eberhard Busch:

"If the only comfort is what Article 1 says it is, then three questions can be inferred from its statement …, which the catechism then in fact addresses one after the other. So it unfolds in detail what is said in Article 1: 1. Why do I need this comfort that is announced to me in advance? Answer: Because I am in *misery!*; 2. Who gives me this comfort? Answer: The God who *redeems* me out of my misery!; 3. What effect does this comfort bring about? Answer: That for this redemption I am *thankful* to this God! These are the three pieces into which the catechism is divided."

On Misery

The following eight questions on human misery now address the following topics:

First Part:
Misery (q. 3–11)
    Our Sin and God's Law (q. 3–4)
    Our Sin and the Just and Merciful God (q. 5–11)

From the perspective of the strange logic of grace, we recognize how the Heidelberg Catechism reevaluates our understanding of human misery by means of the already announced comfort. With the help of *God's Law* (question 3), and the *Two-fold Law of Love* in particular (question 4), we are enabled to admit that we, finite human beings, are in a miserable situation, brought on by our own sin, from which we cannot free ourselves. Even as Christians we will never be able to be without sin, yet there is not one word we can say about sin abstractly, about sinful human beings in and by themselves apart from our belonging to Christ, the One who paid for our sins. All discussion of sin, therefore, can never be more than the second word following God's first word of grace. We are enabled to confess our sins on the basis of being forgiven in Christ; we do not need excuses or finger-pointing: we have been taken out of the blame game. As strange and maybe even scary as it may sound to our modern ears, recognizing and admitting our own sinfulness is, according to the Heidelberg Catechism, already part of God's graceful and liberating work and can only be understood in connection with it. With these eight questions on human misery (out of, as we know, 129 overall), the Heidelberg Catechism underlines the deathly seriousness of our sin and its consequences, but it does not wallow in it.

On Deliverance

Instead, it moves us on to the second part, our deliverance, the confession that we can and may live despite our sinfulness. Or, to be exact, the catechism points us not simply to our deliverance but to the One who is our Liberator, *Christ the Redeemer and Mediator* (questions 12–20).

Question 20 and 21 constitute a pivotal element, not only within this catechism, but in Reformation theology in general, in dealing with the problem of how we participate in the Christ event. We are engrafted into Christ, says the Heidelberg Catechism, through *True Faith,* and it then goes on to describe this true faith from the perspective of God's grace as sure knowledge and wholehearted trust in God's gifts of sheer grace, which we have come to know in the Gospel. The *content* of this faith is developed subsequently on the basis of the

Apostles' Creed (questions 21–64), as a "summary of our universal and undisputed Christian faith". The Credo is, as we have seen before, one of the main Christian texts used in catechisms and catechesis for centuries. It is interesting to note, though, that the first of the traditional catechetical elements treated in the Heidelberg Catechism is not, as in most other Protestant catechisms, the Decalogue, which was often used in order to convict us of our sin and to direct us towards the Gospel (the so-called "first use of the law"). Even though God's law already played a role in recognizing and admitting our sin, an extensive and elaborated exposition of the law of God based on the Decalogue is yet to come. Instead, the Heidelberg Catechism wants to emphasize first and foremost God's decisive word of grace, our only comfort, by explaining the Creed. The Heidelberg Catechism, therefore, following the Trinitarian structure of the Apostles' Creed itself with its emphasis on Christ the Son, deals accordingly with:

Exposition of the Apostles' Creed (q. 26–64)
First Article: "God the Father and our creation" (q. 26–28)
Second Article: "God the Son and our deliverance" (q. 29–52)
Third Article: "God the Holy Spirit and our sanctification" (q. 53–64)

And yet again, it becomes obvious how elaborately this catechism has been structured and devised, always with God's grace *and* the believers "benefit and comfort" in mind: each of these three doctrinal teachings is linked immediately with *our* story as the ones belonging to the graceful God. The doctrine of the Trinity is explained, of course, in a theologically and doctrinal sound way as "sure knowledge", but it is at the very same time also explained as a doctrine that is directly related to us, *our* creation, *our* deliverance, and *our* sanctification, and in which we can "trust wholeheartedly". This conjunction becomes even clearer during the course of the next 44 questions, when the catechism repeatedly asks how some theological knowledge *helps us* (question 28), *benefits us* (questions 36, 43, 45, 49, 51), *comforts us* (questions 52, 57), *does us good* (question 59), *reminds and assures us* (questions 69, 75).

As noted before, we would miss the point here, though, if we would understand all these references to help, benefit, and comfort

from an exclusively anthropological perspective. The Heidelberg
Catechism is, of course, concerned with what human beings ultimately need, but this is not the starting point. The catechism does
not start with our needs first, and asks backwards from there how
God may help us out. Rather, the catechism intends to convey the
message, which had been emphasized so emphatically by John Calvin
in the opening chapter of his famous work, the *Institutes of Christian Religion,* namely that there is no knowledge of God apart from
knowledge of ourselves, *and* no knowledge of who we are apart from
who God is. In other words: we know ourselves as the ones created,
justified, and sanctified by God, and we know God as our Creator,
Savior, and Sanctifier. Question 26 illustrates this understanding
quite exemplary when it explains that believing in "God, the Father
almighty, creator of heaven and earth" means that we believe that
God is, because of Christ the Son, *our* God and Father, and that we
trust God to provide us with whatever we need. Why is that? Not
because of who we are, and what we do and need, but because of
who *God* is, what *God* does and wills. Said with the almost poetic
phrasing of question 26:

> Q. 26:
> God is able to this because he is almighty God,
> and desires to do this because he is a faithful Father.

This, again, is an expression of the strange logic of grace: the almighty
God who created, upholds, and rules all of creation is our faithful
Father providing us with all we need, not because we would deserve
it, but because the good God of grace desires it. Just like the first
question did, we are once more directed not to primarily and exclusively look at our own comfort, but above and first of all at the One
who is our Comforter. Here as well as will be the case throughout
the catechism over and over again, the fundamental concern of the
Heidelberg Catechism is spelled out in different ways: who God is
as the One who acted in Christ for human beings.

 To be sure, this fundamental concern applies not only to the
first two articles of the Creed, the work of God the Father and God
the Son, but equally so to the third article on the Holy Spirit (ques-

tions 53–64). The Holy Spirit is confessed, firstly, as being eternal God with the Father and the Son, and, secondly, as being given to us, to make us share in Christ, to comfort us and to stay with us forever (question 53). The Reformed tradition has often, and sometimes rightly so, been accused of neglecting the doctrine of the Holy Spirit, even of being a "spiritless" church. The Heidelberg Catechism, though, can definitely not be accused of being spiritless. Not only are the Holy Spirit and the work of the Spirit present throughout the whole Heidelberg Catechism, but are explicitly named in pivotal places where the Heidelberg Catechism looks at our being engrafted into Christ. All that has been said above about the believers' "benefit", "assurance", "help", and "comfort" are, of course, only synonyms for the work of the Holy Spirit, because this is what Christ's Spirit is sent to do for, on, in and with us.

An overview of the exposition of the Third Article and its subsections highlights the central and fundamental role of the Holy Spirit's work in the believers' lives:

> The Third Article:
> God the Holy Spirit and Our Sanctification (q. 53–64)
>> The Church: Communion of Saints (q. 54–55)
>> Forgiveness of Sins (q. 56)
>> Life Everlasting (q. 57–58)
>> Righteous by Faith Alone (q. 59–64)

One could even argue, and many scholars do, that not only the immediately following section of the catechism (questions 65–82; treating the Holy Sacraments and including more than one third of the references to the work of the Holy Spirit!) and the third part on the life of Gratitude (to which we are restored by the Spirit, question 86) should be seen as part of the explanation of the doctrine of the Holy Spirit, but that in fact all of the Heidelberg Catechism could be understood as a "pastoral exposition of the Spirit's work" (Daniel Hyde). Resuming our contemplations on the strange logic of grace, we would have to speak about how, by the graceful work of the Holy Spirit, we are enabled to believe and trust in Christ, the Mediator and Redeemer, are engraved into Christ by true faith, and are gathered together as God's community, receiving the "gifts of sheer grace" of the triune God: forgiveness of sin, life everlasting and righteousness.

Recalling what we have said about the historical disputes surrounding the genesis of the Heidelberg Catechism, it comes as no surprise to see how those interpretations of the work of the Holy Spirit for the sake of the believers are described in great and compassionate detail in the following section on the Sacraments (questions 65–82). Already in the introductory questions of this section (questions 65–66), the Heidelberg Catechism emphasizes the purpose of the sacraments through the lenses of the Holy Spirit working for our sake in confessing that the Holy Spirit does not only create true faith in our hearts through the preaching of the gospel, but also confirms this faith by the use of the sacraments. Sacraments, therefore, as visible signs and seals make us understand the promise of the gospel more clearly *and* seal this promise. The whole section on the sacraments is concerned, once more, with the logic of grace, or as question 66 and 67 put it, with explaining *God's gospel promise* as granting us forgiveness of sins and eternal life *by grace* because of Christ's one sacrifice as the only ground of our salvation. A genuine, profound, and systematic understanding and presentation of the doctrine of the Sacraments is understood here not as an end in itself, though it undoubtedly was of high importance to the catechism's authors; it is presented for the purpose of proclaiming the Good News, plain and simply. Particularly with regard to sacraments, sound doctrinal theology matters, the authors were convinced, because it promotes not only better understanding, but greater and deeper trust in God and God's grace. By doing so, it conveys comfort and solace to the terrified and anxious believer. Because of who God is and what God has done and is still doing, theology as God-talk is done here for the sake of the church, for the sake of the troubled believers. Through Christ's once-and-for-all sacrifice on the cross, we personally share in Christ's benefits, and the sacraments are used by the Holy Spirit "to remind and assure us" (questions 69, 75) of this. This sacramental theology is a fine example for the true pastoral theology and perspective we have mentioned before.

Three questions on the "Keys of the Kingdom" (questions 83–85), the tasks of the Christian congregation and their ministers, conclude the second part of the catechism, preparing the transition from "deliverance" to "gratitude" in explaining how the preaching of the Gospel and Christian Discipline open or close the kingdom of heaven according to the behavior, attitude, and convictions of the believers – the message here being, in short, that your moral conduct, your way of life as well as your faith do indeed matter. The logic of grace does not mean that anything goes and you can do as you like, even though your salvation rests on God's work and not your own. With these three questions, we are ushered into the third part dealing with our grateful response to God's salvation. But before moving on, a brief look back at the structure of the second part of the catechism may help us recapitulate the theological reasoning of its understanding of our deliverance:

Second Part:
Deliverance (q. 12–85)
   Christ the Mediator and Redeemer (q. 12–20)
   True Faith (q. 20–21)
   Apostles' Creed (q. 22–64)
      God the Father and Our Creation (q. 26–28)
      God the Son and Our Deliverance (q. 29–52)
      God the Holy Spirit and Our Sanctification (q. 53–64)
         The Church: Communion of Saints (q. 54–55)
         Forgiveness of Sins (q. 56)
         Life Everlasting (q. 57–58)
         Righteous by Faith Alone (q. 59–64)
   The Holy Sacraments (q. 65–85)
      Signs and Seals (q. 65–68)
      Holy Baptism (q. 69–74)
      The Holy Supper of Jesus Christ (q. 75–82)
      Keys of the Kingdom (q. 83–85)

On Gratitude

So far, we have followed the Heidelberg Catechism in its description of the first two aspects of the triple knowledge: misery and deliverance. We have seen, that even with this "human perspective" on our sin and our salvation, the catechism has directed us on every occasion to the One who is our salvation, through whom we are enabled to confess our sin, and through whom we are saved. Even in the third part, entitled "Gratitude", this God-centric orientation is not going to change. In fact, when the catechism now deals with *our* response, we are continuously re-directed back to the One "who makes me wholeheartedly willing and ready from now on to live for him" as the first question confessed right at the beginning. The third part treats two additional Christian texts traditionally used in catechetical material, the Decalogue and the Lord's Prayer, but it displays a distinctive feature by integrated these two text under the heading "Gratitude":

> Third Part:
> Gratitude (q. 86–129)
>   Good Works (q. 86–91)
>   Ten Commandments (q. 92–115)
>   Prayer (q. 116–118)
>   The Lord's Prayer (q. 119–129)

This placement has immense theological meaning: all good works, ethical as well as devotional, are understood as grateful human *responses* to God's gift of grace in Jesus Christ. As Karl Barth observed in his studies on the Heidelberg Catechism, "thankfulness and grace correspond to each other". According to this premise, good works do not earn God's grace, but serve a fourfold purpose: they demonstrate our gratitude, praise God with our whole lives for our deliverance, assure us of our faith by its fruits, and are an invitation to our neighbor to be won over to Christ (question 86). The law, God's commandments, is discussed here not as the law convicting us of our sin, but, as we will later see in detail, as a "rule of true thankfulness and of a Christian life", as Ursinus wrote in his commentary on the Heidelberg Catechism. The subsequent discussion of obedient Christian life and discipleship under the rubric of gratitude develops what has been called an "ethic of gratitude": *thankfulness,* and not fear of God's punishment, motivates the believer to keep the law and do good works out of "a love and delight to live according to the will of

God by doing every kind of good work" (question 90). Thankfulness, though, should not be misinterpreted now as a good work in itself, to be accomplished by the believer. We are indeed the ones who do the good works, but it is *Christ's* Spirit who restores us to his image and enables us to lead a grateful life, although only "in a small beginning" (question 114). The grateful believer is still a sinner (part I), but a forgiven sinner (part II), and as such, her or his answer to God's mercy is to follow God's good law (part III). Since no one can obey God's commandments perfectly (question 114), though, we never stop praying for the grace of the Holy Spirit in order to be renewed (question 115). And with this, the Heidelberg Catechism introduces, in a rather impressive and even surprising way, our devotional "good work": *Prayer* is the most important part of our thankfulness (question 116)! Christian life is not separated into two unconnected sections – here your devout praying life, there your active life of good works. There is not "either – or". Christian life includes both, interrelated, since both are expressions of the believers' gratitude. Grateful prayer prays to the one true God, recognizes the believers' need and misery, and rests on the unshakable foundation that God, because of Christ our Lord, will surely listen to our prayer (question 117). In these two questions, all three central themes of the catechism (misery, deliverance, gratitude), as well as the aspect of comfort from the first question, are bound together with the most intimate practice of a Christian, praying to God. This is exactly what the catechism offers in its exposition of the Lord's Prayer: the last part of the catechism is formulated as a prayer. The language changes from talking *about* God to talking *to* God; the gracious God known in Jesus Christ by the power of the Holy Spirit is directly addressed now by the believer. Again we unmistakably recognize the intention of the catechism to not only teach a doctrinal knowing faith, but also and as much to draw the believers into the practice and performance of a believing faith. The modern German translation from 1997, for example, illustrates this intention by translating the original recurring "this means"-formula in the exposition of the Lord's Prayer's petitions (questions 122–127) with the more expressive wording "with this we pray".

With the last question, we have come back full circle to the first question, when the Heidelberg Catechism concludes the exposition of the Lord's Prayer with explaining the word "Amen", pointing us away from our own desires and wishes towards the One, to whom we belong and who surely listens to our prayers and will never abandon us. That is our only comfort in life and in death.

4. "But Why Are You Called a Christian?" A Brief Commentary on the Heidelberg Catechism[1]

Lord's Day 1 (1–2): Our Only Comfort

Q.1 What is your only comfort in life and in death?
A. That I am not my own, but belong – body and soul, in life and in death – to my faithful Savior, Jesus Christ. He has fully paid for all my sins with his precious blood, and has set me free from the tyranny of the devil. He also watches over me in such a way that not a hair can fall from my head without the will of my Father in heaven; in fact, all things must work together for my salvation. Because I belong to him, Christ, by his Holy Spirit, assures me of eternal life and makes me wholeheartedly willing and ready from now on to live for him.

Q. 2 What must you know to live and die in the joy of this comfort?
A. Three things: first, how great my sin and misery are; second, how I am set free from all my sins and misery; third, how I am to thank God for such deliverance.

A great deal has already been said about this famous first question of the Heidelberg Catechism; and yet there still would be pages, even books to fill in discussing it to a remotely adequate extent. Most important for truly grasping the focus of this question, and with it indeed of the whole catechism, is trying to understand its central term *comfort*. The comfort the Heidelberg Catechism is talking about here is quite different from our contemporary and popular understanding of it. Comfort does not only carry the quite retro-

---

1   The English translation of the Heidelberg Catechism used here is the new translation (without the biblical references) prepared by the *Christian Reformed Church in America,* the *Reformed Church in America,* and the *Presbyterian Church (U.S.A.).*

spective connotation of consoling somebody because of something
that happened in the past, of calming and appeasing distraught people. Rather, a 16th century believer would have associated with it the
semantic field of confidence, assurance, trust, reliance; something
that encourages, sustains, and upholds troubled believers on their
journey through life. Finite human beings find not *a,* but *the only*
comfort in their salvific relationship with their Comforter, in whose
hands they know themselves to be. These are the crucial and decisive words of the first question, the whole catechism, indeed, the
Gospel message: I belong to Jesus Christ – everything else is merely
an exposition of this core truth, in which we clearly recognize the
Reformation emphases on *solus Christus* and *sola gratia,* through
Christ alone and by grace alone.

Because of what God has done for them, once and for all in the
past, and what God continues to do and promises to the believers,
they do not need to fear death – nor life. Sometimes it is harder to
live than to die, as Florence Nightingale once remarked in a letter,
and the authors of the Heidelberg Catechism surely knew this kind
of sentiment. They confess their hope in eternal life, but they do
not try to redirect the believers' attention to the heavenly Everafter
at the expense of all this-worldly concerns and joys: here and now
we are assured of our salvation; here and now we live under God's
providence; here and now we are given Christ's Spirit for serving
God. Two important lines of thought that we will encounter several
times more must be briefly mentioned here. Reformed theology has
often identified Christ's work with the "threefold office" as prophet,
priest, and king. The latter two offices play an important role within
the Heidelberg Catechism, and we meet them already here in the
first question: Jesus Christ as *Priest* paid for our *redemption* with
his own life *(blood),* and, since Christ did not only do something
for us, but also in and to us, Jesus Christ the *King* sends His *Spirit*
to make us *righteous.*

Described with theological terms, the first question brings
together the doctrines of justification, providence, and sanctification,
and in doing so, it describes what it means to be (not to become!)
a Christian from a Trinitarian perspective. We are Christians; we
live and die as Christians, because of the work of the Triune God,

whom we know as Savior, Preserver, and Helper, to use the rather uncommon sequence of the Heidelberg Catechism in placing Christ first. In this sense, the first question could also have been formulated as "*who* is your only comfort in life and in death"?, since it is not so much a doctrinal truth the catechism wants to points us to, but the living God of grace to whom we belong and who belongs to us: "Comfort is the presence of the Comforter" (Karl Barth). The last sentence of the first question spells out in particular what this comfort of belonging means concretely for the way of life of believers. Just as God's grace is no cheap grace, as Dietrich Bonhoeffer emphasized emphatically, so God's comfort in Jesus Christ is no cheap comfort, but instead challenges and encourages us to follow Christ as disciples, as the ones who were bought with a price and are no longer our own [1 Cor 6:19–20]. This "costly comfort" (Allen Verhey) consists therefore not only in consoling us, but equally in endowing us through the Spirit with the strength, courage, and joy to serve God from now on with all our heart, that is, with our whole person. The confession that we are not our own, but belong to Christ, body and soul, in life and in death, claims that in every sphere of our life (the religious as well as the political, economic, social, private, public) we are always Christ's and are called to live as such. In other words: Christian ethics are understood here as part of concretely enjoying the comfort of belonging to God, maybe a somewhat unexpected concept for some, but certainly a typically Reformed understanding.

Question 2 has already been discussed above while analyzing the structure of the catechism according to its triple knowledge, but one more brief remark must be made. We have said before that the Heidelberg Catechism wants to draw the believers into the process and performance of believing, that the catechism understands the whole person with heart and intellect as the addressee of the Good News, and that it wants to teach them not only what to believe, but also to enable them to reflect for themselves, to be accountable for their faith. Correspondingly, the Heidelberg Catechism asks at this point: "what must you *know* …?" Reason, mind, intellect are being addressed here. Being comforted is more than a "good feeling"; it includes perceiving, knowing and understanding as well. And not only that of a theolog-

ically trained caste; *all* believers are invited and summoned to reflect
on their faith and to truly understand their comfort in life and death!
Not necessarily and exclusively in the form of an abstract academic
exercise, to be sure, but as part of their daily Christian existence as
those belonging to Christ who is not only the "Power of God", but
also the "Wisdom of God" [1 Cor 1:24]. Over and over again, the
Heidelberg Catechism will speak about "knowing", "learning", and
"understanding". Evidently it considers one of its principal purposes
as nurturing and promoting not blind assent and affirmation, but a
"faith seeking understanding", as Anselm of Canterbury put it five
centuries prior to the Reformation, an understanding that engages
the mind *and* brings joy and comfort.

Lord's Day 2 (3–5): Human Misery and God's Law

Q. 3 How do you come to know your misery?
A. The law of God tells me.

Q. 4 What does God's law require of us?
A. Christ teaches us this in summary in Matthew 22:37–40: "'You
shall love the Lord your God with all your heart, and with all your
soul, and with all your mind.' This is the greatest and first commandment. And a second is like it: 'You shall love your neighbor
as yourself.' On these two commandments hang all the law and
the prophets."

Q. 5 Can you live up to all this perfectly?
A. No. I have a natural tendency to hate God and my neighbor.

Questions 2 emphasized that in order to enjoy God's comfort we
need to truly know our own misery, the human state in its broken
relationship with God. Even though Reformation theology, and with
it the Heidelberg Catechism, underlines that God in Jesus Christ has
already restored this broken relationship once and for all, that believers as forgiven sinners are already delivered from this state of wretchedness, a pragmatic and reasonable look at our sin is indispensable
if we do not want to gloss over the depth and deathly seriousness of

human misei y. The reality of sin is taken seriously here, because the reality of God's sin-forgiving grace is taken seriously.

How and where do we learn about the seriousness of our sin? The answer of the catechism is clear: not by any form of self-analysis or an evaluation of moral or ethical deficits of our societies, not even by assessing our own actions and thoughts on the basis of the most sophisticated Christian catalogue of virtues and vices. Rather, the *law of God,* and with this, *Godself* tells me. As we have said above, traditionally this understanding of the law has been called the first or spiritual use of the law, where the law not only shows and accuses us of our sin but also guides us to look for forgiveness in Christ. Somewhat exceptional, though, is the fact that Heidelberg Catechism refers not to the Decalogue (which will serve as a rule for grateful living in part III), but to Christ's Twofold Law of Love as the *content* and *substance* of God's law. Love in its twofold appearance as loving God *and* neighbor is required from human beings as God's covenant partners, and negation of love is the cause and consequence of our breaking that covenant. Correspondingly, sin is understood not as an abstract deficiency in moral, religious, or ethical virtues varying from person to person, but fundamentally as a relational reality with concrete negative consequence for every single human being and humankind. No one can escape this state of broken relationship with God and neighbor; no one can live up to the law of God perfectly, all forms of comfortable self-righteousness and complacency are annihilated. Looking at it the other way around: everyone does need God's mercy in Jesus Christ to be brought back into a right and salvific relationship, not only with God, but with other human beings as well.

Part I: Misery

Lord's Day 3 (6–8): Human Nature and Sin

> Q. 6 Did God create people so wicked and perverse?
> A. No. God created them good and in his own image, that is, in true righteousness and holiness, so that they might truly know God their creator, love him with all their heart, and live with God in eternal happiness, to praise and glorify him.
>
> Q. 7 Then where does this corrupt human nature come from?
> A. The fall and disobedience of our first parents, Adam and Eve, in Paradise. This fall has so poisoned our nature that we are all conceived and born in a sinful condition.
>
> Q. 8 But are we so corrupt that we are totally unable to do any good and inclined toward all evil?
> A. Yes, unless we are born again by the Spirit of God.

Who is to blame for this wretched condition of human beings? God creates us good, the catechism insists; human beings are created in the image of God in true righteousness and holiness. So where do we find the origin of our sin? The catechism answers these questions with the biblical story of Adam and Eve and the theological concept of *original* or *inherited sin*. The fall of our first parents has corrupted all succeeding generations, including ours, so entirely that no one of us can escape this sinful condition. In short, with respect to sin, we do not possess a free will; by ourselves, we cannot decide not to sin. Of course, the concept of inherited sin may sound strange, even repulsive to contemporary Christians, and our way of interpreting the biblical fall may differ vastly from that of the Reformation age. This, however, should not obstruct our view on what the catechism wants to say: *all* human beings need Christ, and they cannot save themselves by themselves; no one can contribute anything to her or his own redemption. Strange as it may sound for contemporary ears, for 16th century believers this was indeed the sum of the good news, because this statement is only true together with our confession of Christ as our Savior and Redeemer. We cannot redeem ourselves, and – we do not have to! For people in these times (and maybe in ours as well), the concept of human co-operation was actually a horrific and soul-wrenching concept, because they could never be sure whether they really did enough good works to earn God's grace. This is why the catechism so emphasizes the "only comfort" in its first question; our only comfort is not that we can (and therefore should) escape our sinful condition by our own efforts, or that our condition is not that sinful after all, but that this death-serious, sinful condition has already been healed by Christ. This is the assurance that plays such a central role throughout the whole text.

Even though these three questions and answers seem to provide us with an exclusively negative image of human beings, a careful reading offers a clue of how to understand human beings from the perspective of the Heidelberg Catechism not just as "wicked and perverse people". Question 6 is actually a beautiful description and *positive* affirmation of what human beings are created for: to truly *know* and *love* God, and to live with God in eternal happiness to praise and glorify God. In this description of the aim of human life, we hear and recognize the opening questions ("what is the chief end …"?) of Calvin's Genevan catechism as well as the later Westminster Shorter and Larger Catechism here. Over and over throughout the whole Heidelberg Catechism we will find again this call "Soli Deo Glori" (to God alone be Glory); this axiom of the Reformed reformation is the main recurring theme underlying and determining the whole theological concept of the catechism's understanding of human life. Even though the catechism has stressed the fact that because of our sin we cannot heed to this call all the time, this is not the last word it has to say about the human condition, because it is not the last word God has said about and to human beings. Question 8 reminds us of another effective reality in the life of the believer, because this life ultimately is not confined to the situation of misery and wretchedness: Christian believers are reborn by the Spirit, who makes us "willing and ready *from now on* to live for God" (question 1). For the Heidelberg Catechism, this is true comfort and a cause for great thankfulness.

Lord's Day 4 (9–11): God's Justice

> Q. 9 But doesn't God do us an injustice by requiring in his law what
> we are unable to do?
> A. No, God created human beings with the ability to keep the law.
> They, however, provoked by the devil, in willful disobedience, robbed
> themselves and all their descendants of these gifts.
>
> Q. 10 Does God permit such disobedience and rebellion to go unpun-
> ished?
> A. Certainly not. God is terribly angry with the sin we are born with
> as well as the sins we personally commit. As a just judge, God will
> punish them both now and in eternity, having declared: "Cursed is
> everyone who does not observe and obey all the things written in
> the book of the law."
>
> Q. 11 But isn't God also merciful?
> A. God is certainly merciful, but also just. God's justice demands
> that sin, committed against his supreme majesty, be punished
> with the supreme penalty – eternal punishment of body and soul.

These three questions conclude the first part of the catechism on misery and human sin with contemplations on God's justice and mercy. Who is this God? At first view, the description the catechism gives seems a rather dark one: God is terribly angry and demands punishment for human disobedience and rebellion. God's justice can and will overlook neither the condition of sin we are born with nor the actual sins we commit. God the Just Judge will not ignore the breaking of the salvific relationship of love between humans and God, and between humans and their neighbors – not because some abstract concept of justice would demand it, but because the breaking of this relationship is against God's good intentions for human beings, against what God has created human beings for. This breaking of the covenant with God, this human rebellion, is the cause of our miserable, comfortless situation; it is the reason why we can neither redeem ourselves from this situation nor find any true comfort in it. God's *No* on this human rebellion, however, is, as difficult as it may be to recognize within the wording of the catechism, actually a *Yes* to human beings. By condemning the human-made alienation between God and human beings, God does not ignore or palliate human sin, but takes it as what it is and makes us see the true reality and power of it. We are called not only to accept that our world is in a miserable condition, but we are also called to accept our responsibility for and complicity in this condition. God "has set us free from the tyranny of the devil" (question 1), we are "born again by the Spirit of God" (question 2), and that means in this context, our "response-ability" has been renewed by Christ and his Spirit (Allen Verhey). We are liberated not *from* our responsibilities towards God and neighbor, but liberated *for* them, and part of accepting this responsibility is to genuinely recognize and admit our own sin.

Condemnation and judgment, though, is neither the first nor the last word of God; with this condemnation of sin, God does not forsake or give up on human beings. Taking sin seriously and realistically, holding us accountable for our sins and their deathly consequences, is therefore not only part of God's justice, but also and as much part of God's mercy. Those two attributes of God are not understood to be in opposition; it is not either justice *or* mercy. We have previously met the merciful God, who has already fully paid for all our sins in preceding questions, and it is not a different God whom we now meet. The merciful God is just and the just God is merciful; these two statements cannot be separated without distorting the biblical witness to God. And even though (contemporary?) readers, whose concept of a loving God does not include anything as negative as anger or wrath, may be offended by it, the catechism lays an emphasis on God's anger at this point, because it follows the biblical understanding that God's love and mercy cannot be compromised by unrighteousness, or else they would be no longer *God's* love and mercy.

Part II: Deliverance

Lord's Day 5 (12–15): Satisfaction of God's Justice

> Q. 12 According to God's righteous judgment we deserve punishment both now and in eternity: how then can we escape this punishment and return to God's favor?
> A. God requires that his justice be satisfied. Therefore the claims of this justice must be paid in full, either by ourselves or by another.
>
> Q. 13 Can we make this payment ourselves?
> A. Certainly not. Actually, we increase our debt every day.
>
> Q. 14 Can another creature – any at all – pay this debt for us?
> A. No. To begin with, God will not punish any other creature for what a human is guilty of. Furthermore, no mere creature can bear the weight of God's eternal wrath against sin and deliver others from it.
>
> Q. 15 What kind of mediator and deliverer should we look for then?
> A. One who is a true and righteous human, yet more powerful than all creatures, that is, one who is also true God.

The Heidelberg Catechism depicts the human situation as having arrived at a, in the literal sense of the word, dead end: though humans have been created good and righteous, they all have sinned and continue to sin, and therefore deserve not only God's righteous judgment but also eternal punishment. Yet they cannot do anything at all by themselves to return to God's favor; in not admitting their sin, in relying on their own good works instead of God's grace, they even add daily to their guilt. How, then, is merciful justification of the sinners brought about, so central to the biblical witness and re-emphasized so emphatically by the reformers, if God will comprise neither God's own majesty in righteousness and mercy, nor human responsibility? If there is no indifferent pardon for human beings, how can they be brought back into right relationship with God and neighbor? Who can lift God's curse (question 8) and condemnation from us if *we* are inherently unable to do so? The Heidelberg Catechism does not avoid this, on the face of it, uncomfortable question. On the contrary, it asks outright: if *we* or any substitute sacrifices cannot do it, who can and will pay for our sin, who can and will bridge the gap, who can and will reconcile us with God? Following the logic of the Heidelberg Catechism, the One who is able and willing to act as mediator and deliverer has to be truly human and truly divine. Thus, the doctrine of the two-fold nature of Christ is introduced here not as some form purely theoretical speculation, but as the answer to the burning question from the heart of the believer: how will I be saved?, and as a doctrine conveying God's comfort to the troubled believer.

Lord's Day 6 (16–19): The Mediator and the Holy Gospel

Q. 16 Why must the mediator be a true and righteous human?
A. God's justice demands that human nature, which has sinned, must pay for sin; but a sinful human could never pay for others.

Q. 17 Why must the mediator also be true God?
A. So that the mediator, by the power of his divinity, might bear the weight of God's wrath in his humanity and earn for us and restore to us righteousness and life.

Q. 18 Then who is this mediator – true God and at the same time a true and righteous human?
A. Our Lord Jesus Christ, who was given to us to completely deliver us and make us right with God.

Q. 19 How do you come to know this?
A. The holy gospel tells me. God began to reveal the gospel already in Paradise; later God proclaimed it by the holy patriarchs and prophets and foreshadowed it by the sacrifices and other ceremonies of the law; and finally God fulfilled it through his own beloved Son.

Question 16 recapitulates what has been said about human misery: we are unrighteous sinners and cannot redeem ourselves, but God's justice demands that human nature has to pay. We need a truly human and righteous mediator to pay for our sin, *and* we need a truly divine mediator to bear the weight of God's anger in order to make us right with God again. Here and in the following questions, we encounter a version of a doctrine central to the Reformed tradition, the so-called doctrine of atonement: in Christ' death on the cross and his resurrection, God reconciles the world with Godself, makes "at-one-ment" possible by restoring the relationship between the righteous and merciful God and human sinners. The Heidelberg Catechism emphasizes that the answer to human predicament comes, or rather, has already come in one person, Jesus Christ, whom the reader of the catechism has already met in question 1 as the faithful Savior, who "fully paid for all my sins with his precious blood". Doctrinal faith and personal belief come together as the believer's comfort in these questions; we understand and believe who Jesus Christ is only if we understand and believe who he is *for us,* and vice versa. We will soon see this understanding developed in the exposition of question 21, where the Heidelberg Catechism will deal explicitly with the subject of "true faith". But first the catechism addresses another crucial question, for the Reformation age as for any age: *how* do we know all that? *Where* do we learn about our deliverance? We are reminded here of question 3, where the catechism had asked how we know our *misery.* While the answer of question 3 refers us to God's law, here the catechism speaks of the "holy gospel"; as the law has told me about my sin (question 3), the gospel tells me about my salvation (question 19). The extensive explanation of answer 19 is particularly significant and, yet again, quite characteristic for Reformed theology. We learn about our deliverance from God's holy gospel, which has been revealed to us throughout history, beginning in paradise, continuing over patriarchs and prophets, sacrifices and other ceremonies, and finally in Jesus Christ. This answer is remarkable for, at least, three reasons: a) The catechism stresses the Reformation principle "sola scripura" (Scripture alone), and confesses that all we need to know with reference to our salvation is to be found neither in contemplating nature, in philosophical and theological reasoning, or in analyzing oneself, but in God's Word in form of the Holy Scripture. For the Heidelberg Catechism, there is no other source for redeeming knowledge, and yet it does not confuse "the holy gospel" with the written word or confines it to a book. The holy gospel is what God has revealed throughout history, what has been fulfilled by God's own son, the salvation of human beings; the bible witnesses to this gospel of God's action on behalf of sinful human beings. b) History, human reality in time and space, is understood as the place where the history of salvation takes place, is revealed and proclaimed to humans, from the beginning in the Garden of Eden, throughout Israel's history and culminating in the Christ Event. Historical events as told by the Bible are part of salvation history, and yet they are not self-evident in themselves, but need God's revelation and proclamation in order to be witnesses to the holy gospel. c) The Bible as witness to God's holy gospel and God's law is composed of New Testament as well as Old Testament books, but – and this is yet another Reformed characteristic accent – gospel and law are not assigned to the New and Old Testament, respectively. We find both in each part of the bible, and thus, according to the Heidelberg Catechism, we need and appreciate both parts equally as true witnesses to God's salvific deeds. In no way the Old Testament becomes dispensable or sub-Christian.

Lord's Day 7 (20–23): Salvation and True Faith

Q. 20 Are all people then saved through Christ just as they were lost through Adam?

A. No. Only those are saved who through true faith are grafted into Christ and accept all his benefits.

Q. 21 What is true faith?

A. True faith is not only a sure knowledge by which I hold as true all that God has revealed to us in Scripture; it is also a wholehearted trust, which the Holy Spirit creates in me by the gospel, that God has freely granted, not only to others but to me also, forgiveness of sins, eternal righteousness, and salvation. These are gifts of sheer grace, granted solely by Christ's merit.

Q. 22 What then must a Christian believe?

A. All that is promised us in the gospel, a summary of which is taught us in the articles of our universal and undisputed Christian faith.

> Q. 23 What are these articles?
> A. *I believe in God, the Father almighty, creator of heaven and earth. I believe in Jesus Christ, his only begotten Son, our Lord, who was conceived by the Holy Spirit and born of the virgin Mary. He suffered under Pontius Pilate, was crucified, died, and was buried; he descended to hell. The third day he rose again from the dead. He ascended to heaven and is seated at the right hand of God the Father almighty. From there he will come to judge the living and the dead. I believe in the Holy Spirit, the holy catholic church, the communion of saints, the forgiveness of sins, the resurrection of the body, and the life everlasting. Amen.*

Question 20 turns back briefly to the doctrine of atonement and specifies it to an understanding that has been termed "limited" or "particular" atonement: all have sinned, but not all are saved. Even though the Heidelberg Catechism does not develop an explicit doctrine of election or predestination at this point (it has to say more about God's election within the context of the church in question 54), as many would certainly expect of a Reformed confession, it does teach that Christ's meditorial work is limited to a particular group of believers. Through *true faith* these believers are (passively) incorporated into Christ and (actively) accept Christ's benefits, a decisive sequence. True faith, as a gift of the Holy Spirit, is the precondition and means by which salvation becomes effective in the believer who is united with Christ. It is no coincidence, then, that the Heidelberg Catechism now changes it subject and turn its attention towards the topic of true faith. For all Protestant theologies, this topic is of vital and fundamental importance, as it indicates another center of Reformation theology, another "sola": we are justified sola fide (by faith alone), and no human work, except for Christ's meditorial work, can contribute to our salvation. In question 21, the Heidelberg Catechism provides us with a definition of true faith for which it became famous, not only because its phrasing resonated throughout centuries with Reformed communities all over the world, but just as much so because the Heidelberg Catechism itself is a fine example of this kind of faith as both "sure knowledge" and "wholehearted trust". It does not know of any artificial division or even opposition of intellect and heart, of convinced knowledge and deep assurance, of doctrinally sound and intelligent faith on one side and affectionate and personal belief on the other side. It does not look primarily at human beings for understanding the nature of faith in God, but at what God has done and is still doing, understanding God as the author of this dual-faceted nature of faith. *God* revealed to us all we need to know in Scripture, and *God,* the Holy Spirit, creates in us – by the gospel – a wholehearted trust. These two aspects cannot be separated from each other; God's holy gospel revealed to us is "assured knowledge and knowing assurance" (Fred Klooster) – our comfort. The answer to this question is indeed a carefully woven tapestry of the already mentioned main Protestant principles of Sola Gratia, Sola Fide, Sola Scriptura, Solus Christus (by grace alone, by faith alone, Scripture alone, Christ alone), and encapsulates the Reformation message in a few sentences: in a personal, yet not individualistic perspective, the believer accepts as true with heart and mind to be redeemed and delivered, together with others, by God's free grace because of Christ's work as witnessed to in Scripture – that is true faith.

The Heidelberg Catechism now continues its discussion of true faith with the content of it: *what* do we have to believe? It refers us to the Apostles' Creed as a summary of the gospel promises, claiming over and against all opponents of its time and age its Christian Faith as universal and undoubted. The purpose of the Heidelberg Catechism, as of all Reformation documents, is not to confess a new faith, but to confess the faith anew. In confessing the Apostles' Creed, the catechism asserts its belonging to the one true catholic church of all times and places, and opens the door for ecumenical relations of every kind – as long as the truth of the Christian faith is not obscured by misinterpretations of the holy gospel.

Lord's Day 8 (24–25): The Trinity

Q. 24 How are these articles divided?
A. Into three parts: God the Father and our creation; God the Son and our deliverance; and God the Holy Spirit and our sanctification.

Q. 25 Since there is only one divine being, why do you speak of three: Father, Son, and Holy Spirit?

> A. Because that is how God has revealed himself in his Word: these three distinct persons are one, true, eternal God.

We have already seen how the Heidelberg Catechism connects the three articles of the Apostles' Creed with *us* – *our* creation, deliverance and sanctification. It does not know of any abstract, philosophical, metaphysical, or even theological God-concept apart from the God who has acted and is still acting in, on, and for us. The starting point for confessing the doctrine of God is no academic or metaphysical proof for the existence of God, no extensive list of the attributes of God, no scholarly theories about essence and nature of the Divine Being, but *God* who acts and makes Godself known in these acts. We know and meet God not because of our intellectual reasoning or devout contemplation, but because of God's revelation in God's Word; we know God not as an object of human study, but as an acting subject. All our prefabricated, human-made concepts, theories, and theologies are thus challenged by God's revelation as the One who is our Father, Deliverer, and Sanctifier. This is *who* God is – for us and in Godself. There is no other God than this God, and God is no other than this one; we need not fear any form of hiddenness of God who could be and act differently from the one whom God revealed to us. The doctrine of the trinity, which is addressed here even thought the term "trinity" is not used for catechetical and didactical reasons, is thus understood as a basis for our comfort and assurance, since we experience and know God to be three in one *for and with us,* because God discloses Godself to us as three distinct persons who are one, true, eternal God. We have already seen this understanding of the Christian faith as essentially Trinitarian faith in question 1, where the discussion of our "only comfort in life and death" involves all three persons of the trinity. Following the Heidelberg Catechism, therefore, we divide the Apostles' Creed in three parts and speak about three persons, because we believe in God the Father who created us, God the Son who delivered us, and God the Holy Spirit who sanctifies us, yet as one God and one faith which are directly connected with our life. In the Heidelberg Catechism there is no dividing line between creed and the life of the believer in its intellectual, religious, and ethical dimensions; all creedal statements on God are intimately related to the believer's actual life because in Christ, the believer has been brought back into a right and salvific relationship with God. At this point, we may want to recall the fact that the Apostles' Creed with its three articles is actually discussed within the second part of the catechism, which is concerned with "Our Deliverance".

The First Article: God the Father

Lord's Day 9 (26): God, Father and Creator

Q. 26 What do you believe when you say, "I believe in God, the Father almighty, creator of heaven and earth"?

A. That the eternal Father of our Lord Jesus Christ, who out of nothing created heaven and earth and everything in them, who still upholds and rules them by his eternal counsel and providence, is my God and Father because of Christ the Son. I trust God so much that I do not doubt he will provide whatever I need for body and soul, and will turn to my good whatever adversity he sends upon me in this sad world. God is able to do this because he is almighty God and desires to do this because he is a faithful Father.

The intimate relation between creedal statements and the believer's life in the Heidelberg Catechism, its understanding of faith as assured knowledge and knowing assurance, finds a beautiful expression in the catechism's exposition of the first article of the Apostles' Creed, praised by many as one of the magnificent theological gems of the catechism. In a time when sovereigns reigned in an autocratic manner, understanding themselves as absolute rulers of their subordinated subjects instituted by the grace of God, the Heidelberg Catechism confesses God to be almighty ruler and simultaneously faithful parent, our God *and* Father. Let us begin, however, with the beginning, not only of this answer but also of the theological reasoning applied here, which is inherently Christological: the first thing we have to say and confess about the first person of the trinity is that God is the eternal Father of our Lord Jesus Christ. We do not confess any detached, distant, or neutral creator deity, but the eternal Father of our Lord

Jesus Christ; with this Christological key, creation and redemption cannot and may not be separated. In our being made righteous and brought back into a right relationship with God, we recognize that this just and merciful God did not only bring everything into being, but reigns and sustains all of creation – including us – to this day. At this point the Heidelberg Catechism makes an assertion that would seem like human hubris if our union with Christ is not taken as the foundation and origin of it: the almighty God, creator and ruler, eternal Father of Christ, is *our* Father, who cares for us as whole human beings, with body and soul, and who rules everything for our eternal and temporal benefit. Question 120 will take up this theme again in interpreting the first line of the Lord's Prayer, speaking of our "childlike reverence and trust" with which we expect everything good from God who "through Christ has become our Father". Past, present, and future of humans are encompassed by God's parental love for God's children, because of what God *can* do and *desires* to do – the almighty God is our faithful Father.

The doctrine of creation out of nothing and the doctrine of providence (teaching God's continuing involvement with all of creation in preserving, sustaining, and governing it) are related intimately to each believer's life as we will see in question 28. Already here, though, we observe how the Heidelberg Catechism's inherent certitude of faith finds its expression not only as an objective presentation of information on God, but also the resulting trust of the believer in the form of confidence and assurance in the midst of distress. We encounter a confidence and assurance in this answer that allows for no escape into any form of otherworldliness of church and believers, and that does not rest upon human optimism, belief in progress, or one's own powers and capabilities, but solely on God, who is our only comfort in this life here on earth and beyond it, and who makes us willing and ready to live for God from now on (question 1).

Lord's Day 10 (27–28): God's Providence

Q. 27 What do you understand by the providence of God?
A. The almighty and ever present power of God by which God upholds, as with his hand, heaven and earth and all creatures, and

so rules them that leaf and blade, rain and drought, fruitful and lean years, food and drink, health and sickness, prosperity and poverty – all things, in fact, come to us not by chance but by his fatherly hand.

Q. 28 How does the knowledge of God's creation and providence help us?
A. We can be patient when things go against us, thankful when things go well, and for the future we can have good confidence in our faithful God and Father that nothing in creation will separate us from his love. For all creatures are so completely in God's hand that without his will they can neither move nor be moved.

Everything we encounter, good and bad, life-giving and life-threatening, we receive not by chance or from fate, but from God our Father – a confession that is one of the most difficult to make at any time and everywhere. The authors of the Heidelberg Catechism and their contemporaries certainly knew of the heights, but particularly of the depths of life to an extent many of us may not even be able to imagine: deadly diseases and epidemic plagues, hunger and poverty, and drought periods and flooding were daily fare in those days. Human life was experienced as being continuously threatened, but also, simultaneously, as being nurtured and sustained by nature. Many tried to make sense of these contrasting experiences by reverting to various forms of superstition or resigning to a supposedly unfavorable fate and destiny. Against this kind of attitude, the Heidelberg Catechism sets its knowledge of a faith trusting God as the good parent in each and every situation of life. The doctrine of providence, therefore, is no spiritual, religious, or scientific explanation for adverse or favorable circumstances we may encounter in our lives, but intrinsically an article of faith. It is no intellectually satisfying answer to the question of theodicy (how God can be understood as just and good on the evidence of all evil and suffering in the world), but remains a leap of faith. Now we do not see, know, and understand fully what is happening in our lives and in the life of others, but in Christ we see, know, and understand *who* this God is, who is our creator and redeemer, and who will not let go of us under any circumstance. This defiant, hopeful, and courageous attitude towards all adversities of life does not ignore or deny the bad things in life, but trusts in God to make all things right eventually. It does not give us answers to all questions, but leads us to the praise of God. Thus the knowledge of God's good creation and continuing providence offers us in no way a cause for escapism, but helps us to remain patient, thankful, and confident in all situations of life, as question 28 puts it. As challenging as it is to remain patient in adversities and confident in view of an uncertain future, the Heidelberg Catechism also provides us with another challenging concept that many of us may have even greater problems with: to be thankful when things go well means to look not at ourselves, but at God for the source of all success, all achievements, all good things we experience and encounter – a truly sobering attitude in a society of "self-made people".

Patience, thankfulness, and confidence are the key-words in this answer preventing us from misinterpreting the Heidelberg Catechism's intention: a confident patience and a confident thankfulness do *not* result in passive acceptance and indifference, but, on the contrary, in an active, engaged, and obedient thankfulness as we will see in part III in greater detail. The doctrines of creation and providence teach us that *God* is engaged in this world and will neither let go of it nor let evil and sin have the last word; as those who belong to this God we are enabled to serve God and become part of God's mission.

The Second Article: God the Son

After four questions on God the Father, we now proceed to the exposition of the second article on God the Son in no less than 24 questions, reflecting the heavy emphasis on Christology in the Apostles' Creed itself. One third of these 24 questions deal with the *person* of Christ (questions 29–36), while the following 16 contemplate Christ's *work* in suffering and crucifixion (questions 37–44) and in resurrection and exaltation (questions 45–52). Yet person and work of Christ, even though they are to be distinguished, are not to be separated. As we will notice in the subsequent discussion, both are always intimately interrelated: who Christ is has been revealed in his work, and his work is the manifestation of who he is.

Lord's Day 11 (29–30): The Savior

> Q. 29 Why is the Son of God called "Jesus," meaning "savior"?
> A. Because he saves us from our sins, and because salvation should not be sought and cannot be found in anyone else.
>
> Q. 30 Do those who look for their salvation in saints, in themselves, or elsewhere really believe in the only savior Jesus?
> A. No. Although they boast of being his, by their actions they deny the only savior, Jesus. Either Jesus is not a perfect savior, or those who in true faith accept this savior have in him all they need for their salvation.

The Heidelberg Catechism begins its interpretation of who Christ is with a set of four questions exploring the meaning of Christ's names and titles "Jesus/Savior" (question 29), "Christ/the Anointed" (question 31), "God's only Son" (question 33), and "our Lord" (question 34). As a consequence thereof, the doctrine of the person of Christ is introduced not as an abstract discussion of a theological or metaphysical principle, but by discussing the person of Christ as the one who can be named and addressed by human beings, who is in relationship with them. Yet the answers to these two first Christological questions appear to be somewhat self-evident, familiar, and unexciting: Jesus, the Savior, saves us from our misery, and salvation is not to be sought and found anywhere else. The question "What's in a name?" is taken quite literally here by the Heidelberg Catechism, and with good reason: the name "Jesus" itself is understood as the confession "he will save his people from their sin" [Mt 1:21]. This is only, however, the first of two parts of the answer, since Jesus is also called Savior, because in him alone salvation is found; there is no other savior and for our own sake, we are called to put our trust nowhere else. Most of us have probably heard and said similar "comfortable" statements, similar interpretations of the Reformation's "Solus Christus" (Christ alone), on many occasions without actually pausing and contemplating this central Christian claim and heart of the gospel. Yet these two questions, combining what we have learned so far about human misery, our need for salvation and our delivery,

actually pose one of the most challenging demands and equally comforting assurances of the Christian tradition in every time and place:
to trust exclusively in Jesus Christ as the only, perfect, and complete
Savior with words *and* deeds. Every context needs an interpretation
of what this claim means concretely in its own situation, and this
translating is indeed one of the major tasks of the Christian church.
We may not actually venerate saints, but possibly we put our trust in
other conceptions of "how to be saved and secure", including popular forms of "do-it-yourself salvation". The Heidelberg Catechism
instructs us to carefully and diligently examine the gospel we are
following in order to recognize whether we really and truly put our
trust in Christ alone, and whether we really and truly give witness
to Christ as our only God and Savior with "heart and mouth and life
and deed", as one of Bach's cantatas is entitled. The catechism reminds
us that "to live for God", as question 1 puts it, is not accomplished by
paying ritualistic lip service or trusting in other sources apart from
God's only Son, Jesus Christ. Employing the strange logic of grace
we have already come to know earlier, though, we turn this negative
statement into a positive one: we need not look elsewhere, because in
Christ God's sovereign grace is given to us freely and in abundance.

Lord's Day 12 (31–32): Christ and the Christians

Q. 31 Why is he called "Christ," meaning "anointed"?
A. Because he has been ordained by God the Father and has been
anointed with the Holy Spirit to be our chief prophet and teacher
who fully reveals to us the secret counsel and will of God concerning our deliverance; our only high priest who has delivered us
by the one sacrifice of his body, and who continually pleads our
cause with the Father; and our eternal king who governs us by his
Word and Spirit, and who guards us and keeps us in the freedom
he has won for us.

Q. 32 But why are you called a Christian?
A. Because by faith I am a member of Christ and so I share in his
anointing. I am anointed to confess his name, to present myself to
him as a living sacrifice of thanks, to strive with a free conscience

> against sin and the devil in this life, and afterward to reign with
> Christ over all creation for eternity.

In questions 31 and 32 we find another theological pinnacle of the whole catechism, and encounter two of its "most important and instructive" questions (Karl Barth). As in an ellipse with two foci, we learn who Christ is for us and who we are as those belonging to Christ, and how we become and live as Christians. In short, we learn about the essence of our Christian identity from a Christological perspective. In addition, these questions provide us with a sort of "mini-dogmatics", a concise summary of the Christian faith as assurance and claim upon our life as it reemerged especially in and through the Reformed branch of the Reformation. With this summary, we are enabled to begin pondering the ever-present, though often ignored central question concerning our Christian identity: why are you called a Christian? As we may recall, two of the main purposes of the catechetical didactics of the Heidelberg Catechism were indeed to teach and guide each believer so that she or he might be able not only to give an account of her or his own personal faith, but also to infer practical implications from doctrinal answers for the Christian life of the believer.

Question 31 provides us with the Christological foundation in a Trinitarian perspective: Christ has been ordained by the eternal Father and anointed by the Holy Spirit; neither his person nor his work is thus rightly understood without these inner-Trinitarian relationships. What has Christ, in Hebrew "the Messiah", been anointed for? Drawing on Old Testament teachings and the covenant history of Israel in a way characteristic for Reformed theology, Christ's mediatorial work is explained with the three offices, or rather more precise: with the one *three-fold office* of prophet, priest, and king. Again we see how the Heidelberg Catechism conceives doctrinal statements as intimately related to believers, since Christ is recognized as *our* chief prophet and teacher, *our* only high priest, and *our* eternal king. This three-fold office, therefore, is no abstract concept, valid and meaningful in itself, but is defined by Christ's intervening *for us* and his being *with us*. Christ has been named prophet, priest, and king for a reason: our salvation, which is understood here correspondingly as the revelation of God's will, our deliverance through Christ's sacrifice and advocating, and Christ's governing through Word and Spirit as well as his maintaining us in his freedom.

But why are *we* called Christians? The very simple and straightforward answer is: because by faith, we share in Christ's anointing. Being a Christian is not, according to the Heidelberg Catechism, the result of human decision, choice or effort; Christian identity is not within the control of the Christian, but a free gift from God. We are Christians because we are united with a person, with Jesus Christ, and thus receive – through Christ and like Christ – the anointment with the Holy Spirit. The very same Spirit given to Christ in order to fulfill his work is given to us without any preconditions; there is no Christian being, Christian life, Christian Church, Christianity without the Holy Spirit. The gift of the Holy Spirit, though, is no possession for the believers to be stored away, but given with a clear intention and purpose: it equips the believers to imitate Christ's three-fold office in and with their own life, and it takes them into Christ's Messianic ministry. To be anointed means, for Christ as for us, to be given a task. As prophets and teachers we all, laity as well the so-called clergy, are called to confess Christ's name with words and deeds, to proclaim the good news, to protest against injustice in any form, to make known the Lordship of Christ over all powers and dominions. As priests we present ourselves as living sacrifices of gratitude, not in earning our redemption, but in giving thanks for it with all of who we are. A quite memorable interpretation of the priesthood of all believers! Most important for our understanding of our kingly office as those sharing in the anointing of Christ is to remember that this office is, just like the other two, defined by Christ's office and therefore no reason for any kind of triumphalism, since it leads us to the cross rather than to a throne. Sharing in Christ's anointment, being a Christian as well as a Christian community, means fighting against sin and the devil and entails active, praiseful, and obedient engagement in and for this world, with a free conscience, not bound by any worldly authority, but answerable to God for our deeds. At the same time, Christians know that they are living in the tension between, on the one hand, the "already" of Christ's victory over sin and evil, and, on the other hand, the "not yet" of the coming kingdom, where they will reign with Christ in eternity. This tension leads each Christian and all Christian communities to assume an attitude that is at the same time deliberately this-worldly *and* hopefully awaiting what is yet to come – or rather, who is yet to come again, Christ our eternal king.

Lord's Day 13 (33–34): The Son of God and Our Lord

Q. 33 Why is he called God's "only begotten Son" when we also are God's children?
A. Because Christ alone is the eternal, natural Son of God. We, however, are adopted children of God – adopted by grace through Christ.

Q. 34 Why do you call him "our Lord"?
A. Because – not with gold or silver, but with his precious blood – he has set us free from sin and from the tyranny of the devil, and has bought us, body and soul, to be his very own.

The catechism now turns to the interpretation of the last two of Christ's titles mentioned in the Apostles' Creed, namely "Son of God" and "Lord", which are, again, discussed not as abstract concepts in themselves, but in their relevance and importance for the believer as defined through Christ's work. Accordingly, the catechism does not place too much emphasis on a doctrine of divine sonship except for stating Christ's unique relation to God the Father as the only natural son from all eternity, only to be continued with the explanation of our adoption. Indeed, Christ alone is the only Son of God, the eternal and faithful Father, but because of this Christ and of this Father, we are, by grace, *adopted children* of God. With this strong familial metaphor, the Heidelberg Catechism takes up the Pauline theme of being brought back into the family of God, a variation on the subject of what it means to be saved. Through Christ, the consequences of sin in breaking our relationship to God and one another are undone; God's grace reestablishes us as rightful children of God and members of the family. It is not only the legal aspect of this metaphor that makes it so valuable and meaningful, but also the positive description of Christian life as members of one family, with Christ as our Brother, God as our faithful Father and fellow human beings as *our* and *Christ's* brothers and sisters (see the following question and answer). The doctrine of adoption, thus, emphasizes not only what Christ saved us *from* (our sin and its miserable consequences), but even more so what we are saved *for*: living as the children of God with and for God, whom we are given the right to call "Our Father". And again, our identity as Christians is not so much defined by who or what we are, but by *whose* we are, whom we belong to – and who belongs to us.

This double relationship of belonging is made the subject of the next answer, too. We are Christ's very own, having been bought for a price, and thus the status of "affiliation" (literally: being adopted as a child) has changed: we no longer belong to the devil but to the One, the Mediator, whom we may call *our* Lord now. With many parallels to question 1, even with almost identical expressions, the Heidelberg Catechism describes the term lordship within the meaning of a change in ownership as the result of purchase and deliverance. Unexpectedly, though, the Heidelberg Catechism remains atypically silent on the practical implications of Christ's lordship; it does not even reiterate the closing remarks concerning Christian life from question 1. In addition, the generally human-centered perspective of the Heidelberg Catechism translates in this answer to a rather limited scope of Christ's lordship that is not discussed in any of its aspects reaching beyond human beings – any reference to the all-encompassing kingdom of Christ is missing. Reading those two questions together, though, may offer fresh insights into person and work of Jesus Christ with respect to his lordship, since we will not really understand it as long as we do not integrate into it our knowledge about Christ as our *brother*. Christ's lordship is not defined by our current or past understandings of the term, but by God's work and revelation in Christ.

Lord's Day 14 (35–36): Incarnation

Questions 35 and 36 mark the transition from the catechism's discussion of the person of Christ to the discussion of the work of Christ, both being deliberately interwoven in these two answers as will we see below.

Q. 35 What does it mean that he "was conceived by the Holy Spirit and born of the virgin Mary"?

A. That the eternal Son of God, who is and remains true and eternal God, took to himself, through the working of the Holy Spirit, from the flesh and blood of the virgin Mary, a truly human nature so that he might also become David's true descendant, like his brothers and sisters in every way except for sin.

Q. 36 How does the holy conception and birth of Christ benefit you?

A. He is our mediator and, in God's sight, he covers with his innocence and perfect holiness my sinfulness in which I was conceived.

What we are dealing with in question 35 has appropriately been called the "Christmas Wonder" (Eberhard Busch), and it remains indeed a "wonder" until this day although not for the reason many might assume. The catechism is not at all concerned with the biological aspect of the virgin birth; the wonder of Christmas consists in the miraculous event of the Second Person of the Trinity, the eternal Son of God, becoming human, taking to himself a truly human nature. The incarnation of God, his embodiment in human flesh, is not explained here, but confessed as the work of the Holy Spirit, thus indicating the Spirit's active role in Christ's mediatorial work from the beginning. Incarnation is understood as an act of God's grace for our benefit, so that Jesus might be like us, his brother and sisters; it is a divine gift and not the result of human procreation. In this one human, in the historical Jew Jesus of Nazareth, David's true descendant, God fulfilled God's covenant and united Godself indissolubly with humanity. Our Lord, the prophet, priest, and king, was brought into the world by Mary under very humble conditions, becoming truly human just like us in every way except for sin for a reason. The embodiment of the Second Person of the Trinity in Christ's lowly birth is understood here as the beginning of Christ's work, his active obedience. It is the beginning of Christ's debasement into the *state of humiliation,* which will continue in his suffering, death on the cross, and descent into hell, after which Christ's glorification in his *state of exaltation* in resurrection, ascension, and glorious reigning will be taking place. Significantly, the Heidelberg Catechism inquires at each of these stages of Christ's work in humiliation and exaltation after *our benefit,* how it *benefits us* (questions 35, 43, 45, 51, except for question 49 where the answer speaks about our "assurance"). These "benefit questions" indicate, yet again, that the Heidelberg generally understands both person and work of Jesus Christ, as "for-us-ness". In the case of question 36, the benefit of Christ's conception through the Holy Spirit and birth of the Virgin Mary is understood as Christ's covering our sinfulness as the mediator, which the catechism already discussed earlier in detail, and therefore needs not to be reiterated here.

Lord's Day 15 (37–39): Suffering and Cross

Q. 37 What do you understand by the word "suffered"?
A. That during his whole life on earth, but especially at the end, Christ sustained in body and soul the wrath of God against the sin of the whole human race. This he did in order that, by his suffering as the only atoning sacrifice, he might deliver us, body and soul, from eternal condemnation, and gain for us God's grace, righteousness, and eternal life.

Q. 38 Why did he suffer "under Pontius Pilate" as judge?
A. So that he, though innocent, might be condemned by an earthly judge, and so free us from the severe judgment of God that was to fall on us.

Q. 39 Is it significant that he was "crucified" instead of dying some other way?
A. Yes. By this I am convinced that he shouldered the curse which lay on me, since death by crucifixion was cursed by God.

The above-mentioned "for-us-ness" of Christ is now spelled out further, beginning with Christ's suffering in questions 38 and 39: Christ suffered for us all of his life, and especially at the end under the judge Pilate. The Heidelberg Catechism thus explains the one-line statement ("he suffered under Pontius Pilate") from the Apostles' Creed in several sentences and with particular emphases. While the Apostles' Creed, for instance, moves non-stop from Christmas to Good Friday, the Heidelberg Catechism interprets Christ's suffering as a *life-long,* continuous suffering "from his mother's womb to the grave" (Ursinus, Larger Catechism, question 79), experiencing sufferings of the body in physical pains *and* the soul in spiritual and emotional pains such as rejection, temptation, sorrow, anguish, condemnation, and abandonment. Christ was no impassible and indifferent divine figure, disguised as human being, but a feeling and sensible person, whose sufferings touched his inmost person. In these sufferings of *body and soul,* Christ sustains the anger of God against the sin of all humans, including ours, in order to deliver us, *body and soul,* from condemnation – in this we recognize Christ our Savior and Brother for and with us. And even more, we have not only been acquitted of our guilt, Christ has also acquired for us God's grace, righteousness, and eternal life, which we receive as a free and merciful gift because of Christ's sacrifice. With its once-for-all character, Christ's unique sacrifice is the denegation and rejection of all forms of suffering for meritorious purposes: we cannot and we need not suffer for our deliverance, our being reconciled with God. Even in this very solemn section of the catechism with its discussion of suffering and death, its main theme, the comfort of the believer, shines through all its contemplations of Christ's work. At the same time, this comfort also exposes our own efforts for self-redemption and self-justification as what they really are: reliance and trust in ourselves and our own capacities as a form of self-idolatry, and an abnegation of our complete and absolute belonging to God. This belonging to God, though, is not understood to be the result of suffering and cross of Christ, as if God's wrath had to be appeased through a sacrifice before God could love human beings again. Just the opposite, in suffering and cross, God's love and mercy deal effectively with human misery and sin, Godself in Christ bears the righteous and just No that turns into a gracious and merciful Yes to human being. Grace is not exercised *instead* of justice, but *through* justice; and justice is exercised by exalting grace (Karl Barth). Here we find another example of what has been called the strange logic of grace for which the Heidelberg Catechism in particular and Reformation theology in general have been known.

After discussing the meaning of Christ's suffering, the catechism now turns to the historical person of Pilate, who is besides Mary and, of course, Jesus Christ, the only other human being mentioned in the Apostles' Creed. The Heidelberg Catechism is not so much interested at this point in the historical dating of Christ's trial before and condemnation by Pilate, thus anchoring the human person Jesus in a particular time and place, but in explaining the theological reason for Christ's condemnation by an earthly judge. The innocent, sinless Jesus Christ, truly God and truly human, took on himself the judgment so that we, justly deserving not only earthly but also eternal judgment, might walk free. Luther called this the "joyous exchange": Christ takes over what is ours (sin and condemnation), and we are given what would be rightly his (righteousness and eternal life); a "reversal of all things" (John Calvin) has taken place. In shouldering the cross, Christ shouldered the curse that lay on us because of our sin – a strong and expressive metaphor. In fact, more than a mere metaphor, for the Heidelberg Catechism follows the biblical understanding of crucifixion as not only one of the most excruciating, humiliating, and brutal forms of execution, but also as ignominious and scandalous death – cursed by God. Cross and death by crucifixion are, therefore, not coincidental or dispensable, since only by them we recognize that the true and unfathomable depth of our misery, of our being accursed, has been dealt with in Christ's death on the cross once and for all. Consequently, any theology of the cross, any theology of Good Friday has to be developed around this central statement: God in Christ for us and with us.

Lord's Day 16 (40–44): Death and Descent to Hell

Q. 40 Why did Christ have to suffer death?
A. Because God's justice and truth require it: nothing else could pay for our sins except the death of the Son of God.

Q. 41 Why was he "buried"?
A. His burial testifies that he really died.

Q. 42 Since Christ has died for us, why do we still have to die?

A. Our death does not pay the debt of our sins. Rather, it puts an end to our sinning and is our entrance into eternal life.

Q. 43 What further benefit do we receive from Christ's sacrifice and death on the cross?
A. By Christ's power our old selves are crucified, put to death, and buried with him, so that the evil desires of the flesh may no longer rule us, but that instead we may offer ourselves as a sacrifice of gratitude to him.

Q. 44 Why does the creed add, "He descended to hell"?
A. To assure me during attacks of deepest dread and temptation that Christ my Lord, by suffering unspeakable anguish, pain, and terror of soul, on the cross but also earlier, has delivered me from hellish anguish and torment.

Even though question 40 takes up the already covered material of Christ's dying to pay for our sins, it still is worthwhile to dwell on two issues of it: the reference to God's *truth* in combination with God's justice, and the explicit use of the title Son of God for Jesus Christ in this answer. Let us first look briefly at the phrase *God's truth,* which is only mentioned twice in the Heidelberg Catechism (here and again in question 122). In this context, God's truth refers to God's proclamation from the beginning in paradise that the consequence of sin is death. It is brought up here to emphasize that God does not lie, but is always and unalterably true to God's own word in both forms: as word of redemption *and* as word of condemnation. Without the death of Jesus Christ, God's truth would have been violated as much as God's justice, but the death of the *Son of God,* of the Second Person of the Trinity, bore the consequences for our sins, and thereby ensured that God's justice and truth, as well as God's love and mercy, remain inviolate. This is the holy gospel of Good Friday: the Son of God, Godself, died for us! Really and truly died for us, as the next question stresses by referring to Christ's burial, which is understood as a *testimony* to bring us comfort and assurance, not only for our life, but for our dying as well. With question 42, the catechism aims at changing the believer's attitude towards her or his own death: since we cannot and do not have to pay for our sin, not even with our own death, we need not be afraid of it. Because of Christ's sacrifice, our death has lost its final terror for us. All of us will really, truly die, but this will not be the end of our relationship with God. On the contrary, in our dying, our sinning comes to an end, and we will enter into a state of perfect blessedness (question 58); that is what the catechism confesses as our only comfort in life and death/dying. But there is more. In addition to changing our attitude towards our dying, Christ's death has life-changing and life-giving consequences here and now. Again, the Heidelberg Catechism is concerned with concrete and practical implications of doctrinal statements and their relevance for Christian life, interpreting the benefit we receive from Christ's sacrifice as *our death:* our old sinful, miserable, self-justifying, self-idolizing, God-and-neighbor-hating selves were crucified, died and were buried with Christ. Accordingly, we have already been freed from the domination of evil desires; we are already set free from the tyranny of the devil over our body and soul (cf. question 1) and belong to our faithful Savior. In dying with Christ, our life has changed; new life is given in that we already now are enabled to present ourselves as sacrifices of gratitude to God (cf. question 32). Redemption and deliverance lead directly towards and into the Christian life of gratitude; part III will cover this extensively, but we can recognize already at this point, once more, how carefully all questions, sections, and parts are designed and interwoven in order to theologically correlate with each other.

Question 44 concludes the catechism's section on Christ's so-called state of humiliation in incarnation, suffering, death and finally his descent to hell, which constituted a highly controversial issue in theological discourse. The Heidelberg Catechism offers no theological reasoning for why and how Christ descended to hell and what he did there; instead, it interprets the Apostles' Creed intention in adding this line as a quintessentially pastoral one. Christ's descent is full of consolation for us, as Calvin said, because this way, God made our affair God's own in experiencing our weakness so as to better to support us in our weakness. In Christ's life-long suffering, and in particular in suffering the horrors of the cross, we therefore recognize not only God in Christ *for* us but also God in Christ *with* us; his suffering for us includes his suffering with us.

Lord's Day 17 (45): Resurrection

Q. 45 How does Christ's resurrection benefit us?
A. First, by his resurrection he has overcome death, so that he might make us share in the righteousness he obtained for us by his death. Second, by his power we too are already raised to a new life. Third, Christ's resurrection is a sure pledge to us of our blessed resurrection.

Proceeding from Good Friday to Easter Sunday, the catechism now turns to Christ's resurrection as the first part of Christ's exaltation, not by explaining the meaning of resurrection in itself, but by delineating a threefold description of the benefits we receive from it. With that, the Heidelberg Catechism begins to indirectly make *our exaltation,* too, the subject of the subsequent eight questions. In Christ, God came down to be for us and with us in the depth of human misery, and in Christ, God is taking us home to be with God. The Easter resurrection, therefore, is no abrogation of Christ's sacrifice on the cross, but the fulfillment of it; the God of the resurrection is no other than the God of the crucifixion, and to this God we belong, body and soul, in life and in death. Question 45, therefore, could be understood as a three-dimensional exposition of the first question in the context of the resurrection. It may surprise us, though, that only one question deals Christ's resurrection considering the central importance and theological significance of this event. One explanation might be that the doctrine of the resurrection was not at all controversially debated at that time, neither between differing Reformation branches, nor between Reformation theologies and Roman Catholic theology. (Plus, it was not until two hundred years later that the historicity and factuality of the resurrection was contested by the first so-called "quest for the historical Jesus" in the 18th century.) Even so, this one single question on the resurrection in its three-dimensional composition with its focus on our benefits provides us with a theologically dense, yet pastoral exposition. The benefits we receive unfold in three aspects related to the past, present, and future of our lives as those belonging to God: Christ has overcome death and won righteousness for us; Christ resurrects us already now to new life; in Christ's resurrection we are assured of our own prospective resurrection. The first aspect emphasizes that Christ has not only attained righteousness for us, which would then remain outside of us as a purely descriptive legal status, but that in his defeating death, Christ makes us *share* in his righteousness. We actually become righteous and are not only declared righteous. The second aspect continues this line of thought in confessing that Christ's resurrection has immediate consequences for our present lives: we are already reborn, resurrected to a new life right here and now, to live for God from now on. Christ's resurrection does not only concern our life after death, but gives us "life before death" (Eberhard Busch). Even with the third aspect that speaks about our own future resurrection, the Heidelberg Catechism is not interested in proposing a sort of belief in the hereafter with no connection to our daily life, but interprets Christ's resurrection as a sure pledge that will us provide comfort in spiritual crises. The Easter resurrection, therefore, has brought us back into a right relationship with God for which we have been redeemed, reconciled and made new.

Lord's Day 18 (46–49): Ascension

Q. 46 What do you mean by saying, "He ascended to heaven"?
A. That Christ, while his disciples watched, was taken up from the earth into heaven and remains there on our behalf until he comes again to judge the living and the dead.

Q. 47 But isn't Christ with us until the end of the world as he promised us?
A. Christ is true human and true God. In his human nature Christ is not now on earth; but in his divinity, majesty, grace, and Spirit he is never absent from us.

Q. 48 If his humanity is not present wherever his divinity is, then aren't the two natures of Christ separated from each other?
A. Certainly not. Since divinity is not limited and is present everywhere, it is evident that Christ's divinity is surely beyond the bounds of the humanity that has been taken on, but at the same time his divinity is in and remains personally united to his humanity.

> Q. 49 How does Christ's ascension to heaven benefit us?
> A. First, he is our advocate in heaven in the presence of his Father.
> Second, we have our own flesh in heaven as a sure pledge that
> Christ our head will also take us, his members, up to himself. Third,
> he sends his Spirit to us on earth as a corresponding pledge. By
> the Spirit's power we seek not earthly things but the things above,
> where Christ is, sitting at God's right hand.

As we have just seen, the Heidelberg Catechism devotes, probably contrary to our expectations, just one question on Christ's resurrection, whereas Christ ascension demands a more detailed discussion in four questions. Again we are referred back to the historical controversies that caused Frederick III to commission the work on the Heidelberg Catechism. In particular, we are reminded of the theological debates on the nature of the elements of the Lord's Supper, whether Christ's body and blood is indeed present in them. At the heart of this controversy lie differing understandings of the unity between Christ's humanity and his divinity; questions 47 and 48 will address this issue.

First, however, the catechism explains the meaning of Christ's ascension as the end of Jesus' post-Easter appearances before his disciples who became the witnesses to his ascent into heaven, which is actually described in the passive voice as being taken up: Christ, the incarnate Son of God, is taken home by God the Father. The catechism is, once more, not really interested in the historicity of the event, but in its theological meaning, which the catechism understands as linked to us and our sake. Christ remains there *on our behalf* as question 49 will explain in greater detail. This same Christ, who became human for our sake, died for our sake, descended into hell for our sake, was resurrected for our sake, is the One who will come back as Judge – we await no other.

In questions 47 and 48, the Heidelberg Catechism comes back to the discussion of the two natures of Christ as truly human and truly divine, which has been brought up several times before. This time, though, the catechism is concerned with a particular aspect of it: how the divine nature of the Second person of the Trinity ("the infinite") was never completely contained by the human nature ("the finite"), but remained active beyond ("extra") the human body; a teaching that was later called the *extra-Calvinisticum* (the Calvinistic extra) by Lutheran theologians. From this reasoning the catechism concludes, that though Christ is truly with us in his divinity, grace, majesty, and Spirit, his human nature is not present on earth – in particular not within in the elements of the Lord's Supper. The catechism claims that both natures are and remain, indeed, indissolubly united in the person of Jesus Christ; yet as the divine nature is not limited by the human nature, the human nature is in no way "divinized" and can therefore not participate or communicate in the omnipresence of the divine nature (a Lutheran position called *ubiquity*). This rather scholastic reasoning seems somewhat out of tune with the more pastoral and personal undertone we have encountered so far, but we will later learn how this understanding plays out in its pastoral perspective in the discussion of the Lord's Supper. Already here, though, the theological interest of the Heidelberg Catechism is clear: in emphasizing that neither the divine is transformed into the human nor the human into the divine, the catechism aims at maintaining the distinction between the saving God, who takes on human nature, and human nature being redeemed and taken up by God, united but not mixed in the one Christ. Only in this way Jesus Christ, as our brother in his humanity, is our sure pledge, assurance, and comfort, since our human nature also remains completely human and "un-divinized".

With this observation, we have already moved into the discussion of the benefits we receive from Christ's ascension, and encounter another one of those "benefit-questions". With these questions, the Heidelberg Catechism tries to get to the foundation of our comfort springing from the Christ event in each of its aspects, not always introducing new insights, but repeatedly taking up already familiar material and illuminating it from another perspective. Once more the benefits are developed within a three-fold perspective, beginning with Christ as our advocate in heaven "who continually pleads our cause with the Father", as question 31 formulated with reference to Christ's priestly office. Secondly, Christ's ascension is, as was his resurrection, our guarantee that also we as the members of Christ's body will be taken up to God. In Christ, and here the discussion from questions 47 and 48 comes to fruition, we have *our own flesh*, and no divinized form of a human, in heaven as a sure pledge. This pledge, however, does not remain far away and apart from us in heaven, but is also sent to us down on earth in the person of the Holy Spirit, Christ's Spirit, and it does not remain a solely future pledge, since in the work of the Holy Spirit we are redirected towards our Lord and Brother in Heaven already here and now.

Lord's Day 19 (50–52): The Glory of Christ and the Last Judgment

Q. 50 Why the next words: "and is seated at the right hand of God"?
A. Because Christ ascended to heaven to show there that he is head of his church, the one through whom the Father rules all things.

Q. 51 How does this glory of Christ our head benefit us?
A. First, through his Holy Spirit he pours out gifts from heaven upon us his members. Second, by his power he defends us and keeps us safe from all enemies.

Q. 52 How does Christ's return "to judge the living and the dead" comfort you?
A. In all distress and persecution, with uplifted head, I confidently await the very judge who has already offered himself to the judgment of God in my place and removed the whole curse from me. Christ will cast all his enemies and mine into everlasting condemnation, but will take me and all his chosen ones to himself into the joy and glory of heaven.

With these three questions on Christ's glory and judgment, the Heidelberg Catechism concludes its exposition of the Second Article of the Apostles' Creed, ending not only with one of its Christological "benefit questions", but with a question asking about the comfort of this teaching. This is remarkable insofar as it is the first time after the introductory questions 1 and 2 that the Heidelberg Catechism actually makes use of this central term again, marking this question as a particularly important one in the course of the catechism for two reasons. First, the issue of Christ's second coming and the so-called Last Judgment was at the heart of theological controversies that triggered the Reformation and kept people anxious and troubled; if there was any single issue in people's spiritual life that called for a mighty comfort, this might have been it. Second, at this transition from the Second Article that explicated the *content and implications* of our comfort (Christ saving work in being for and with us), to the Third Article, which explicates the *way of our receiving* this comfort (our sharing in Christ's benefits through the work of the Holy Spirit), the term "comfort", which is taken up subsequently in questions 53, 57 and 58, denotes the centrality of the work of the Holy Spirit as Christ's Spirit on, in, and for us.

Let us, though, first look at question 50 with its strong emphasis on Christ's *present* lordship. After working through Christ's humiliation and exaltation in the whole course of the Christ event, we now encounter the incarnated, crucified, resurrected, and ascended Christ, sitting at the right hand of God, as the *head of his church,* as our head. Paying careful attention to the formulation of the Heidelberg Catechism, we notice an important dissolution of boundaries here: Christ's lordship is not confined to the walls of the church, since through him, the Father rules *all things,* church and world. The church, therefore, does not stand above or against the world in any sense, but stands together with it under the immediate and all-encompassing reign of Christ which is understood as the *glory of Christ.* And since this Christ is always understood in the Heidelberg Catechism as God for and with us, it does not come as a surprise that even this attribute of Christ's glory is understood correctly only in its relation to us, since it is no other glory than the glory of the crucified and risen Lord. Thus the question about our benefits unfolds quite plausibly from what has been said before. Christ, the head, continues his salvific work from sitting at the right hand of God in granting us his gifts of grace through the work of the Holy Spirit, and in defending and keeping us safe; another interpretation of what it means to belong to our faithful savior in life and death. Before interpreting the term "enemies" prematurely only with reference to human foes and opponents, a look at question 127 might help broadening the picture, since there "our sworn enemies" are interpreted as "the devil, the world, and our own flesh".

Question 52 turns towards the future, which as such is the comfort of the church. Why? Because the future of the believers, individually and as a community, is not a veiled mystery, but will bring the second coming of the Lord, the one who has already come is the very same one who will come again. Maybe surprisingly for some, the coming of the *Judge* is accordingly understood as true comfort, since this judge is the One who was judged for us, who took our curse on himself. This judge will lift us up with him, condemning all his and our enemies to eternal perdition.

The Third Article: God the Holy Spirit, the Church, and the Gifts of Grace

Lord's Day 20 (53): The Holy Spirit

> Q. 53 What do you believe concerning "the Holy Spirit"?
> A. First, that the Spirit, with the Father and the Son, is eternal God. Second, that the Spirit is given also to me, so that, through true faith, he makes me share in Christ and all his benefits, comforts me, and will remain with me forever.

After 24 questions on person and work of the second person of the Trinity, Jesus Christ, this one single question on the Holy Spirit seems like a rather disappointing anticlimax in its brevity and conciseness – although the Apostles' Creed itself is even less detailed in merely confessing belief in the Holy Spirit without expounding it at all. As we have noted above in chapter 3, however, this is by far not all the Heidelberg Catechism has to say about the work of the Holy Spirit; on the contrary, the work of the Holy Spirit runs like a golden thread through the fabric of the whole catechism, and is present at all main intersections. So far, the Heidelberg Catechism has referred to the work of the Holy Spirit in discussing how the Holy Spirit, together with the Father and the Son, is one, eternal, true God (question 25); how Christ's Spirit assures us of our eternal life, gives new life, governs us and abides with us, creates wholehearted trust in us through the gospel, is the earnest of our salvation on earth and redirects us towards heaven (questions 1, 8, 12, 21, 47, 49); how Christ was conceived and anointed by the Holy Spirit (questions 23, 31, 35); how through the Spirit we receive the gifts of grace (question 51). In a sense, we look back in question 53 at what God has done, we look at what God is still doing and will do for, on, in, and with us. Question 53 is, then, not a conclusive and extensive treatment of the work of the Holy Spirit, but a concise, yet immensely meaningful summary of it, a binding together of the different strands that have been woven into the various doctrinal considerations. The fact that Lord's Day 20 is devoted to this one particular question further underlines its theological significance.

So what does the Heidelberg Catechism has to say about the Holy Spirit in its summary? The first part repeats what has already been stated in the introduction to the Apostles' Creed (question 25): God the Holy Spirit is eternal God, not less God than God the Father and God the Son, not separated from the two other persons, but together with them the One true God. That means the work of the Holy Spirit is the work of *God;* it is not separated from the work of the Father and the Son, even though the Spirit's works has its unique features that the Heidelberg Catechism described as "sanctification" in question 24. Sanctification is *God's* work in the Christian believer's life resulting in growth in grace and holiness; the "being-made-holy" of human beings is the consequence of the Spirit's work, not of human effort or works. Thus the recurring emphasis on the divinity of the Spirit – with the Father and the Son – is crucial in understanding God's gracious relationship to human beings in its three-fold dimensions of creation, redemption, and sanctification as the one work of the triune God. As we will later see again in the third part of the catechism and the discussion of the life of gratitude, the Heidelberg Catechism, accordingly, never separates justification (how we become righteous before God) and sanctification (how we live holy lives as righteous people).

The description of the Holy Spirit's work in the second part of question 53 is a restatement of what has already been said several times so far, and we could recapitulate it with the phrasing from question 32: but why are you called a Christian? The simple answer to this question is: We are called Christians because of the work of the Holy Spirit. Vice versa, the answer to the question of what we believe concerning the Holy Spirit is equally simple: the Holy Spirit makes us Christians – in receiving the Spirit, true faith is created in our hearts (see also question 65) and through this faith, we are made participants in Christ and receive God's gift of grace. The Holy Spirit, thus, is the "personal, intimate, comforting bond of union between Christ and his people." (Daniel R. Hyde). We are Christians because of the Holy Spirit, who is our eternal Comforter, and, accordingly, our Christian lives can in no aspect be understood apart from the Holy Spirit, who "makes us wholeheartedly willing and ready from now on to live for God" (question 1). "I believe in the Holy Spirit", then, translates into I believe in God, who "in Christ comes to be in relationship with us, and in the Holy Spirit brings us into relationship" (Eberhard Busch); that is, indeed, the comfort of belonging to Christ. Of course, since question 53 is neither the starting nor the endpoint of the exposition of the faith in the Holy Spirit, we will encounter the work of the Third Person of the Trinity in about twenty more questions of the catechism; the next one being but one of them.

Lord's Day 21 (54–56): The Communion of Saints and Forgiveness of Sins

Q. 54 What do you believe concerning "the holy catholic church"?
A. I believe that the Son of God through his Spirit and Word, out of the entire human race, from the beginning of the world to its end, gathers, protects, and preserves for himself a community chosen for eternal life and united in true faith. And of this community I am and always will be a living member.

Q. 55 What do you understand by "the communion of saints"?
A. First, that believers one and all, as members of this community, share in Christ and in all his treasures and gifts. Second, that each member should consider it a duty to use these gifts readily and joyfully for the service and enrichment of the other members.

Q. 56 What do you believe concerning "the forgiveness of sins"?
A. I believe that God, because of Christ's satisfaction, will no longer remember any of my sins or my sinful nature which I need to

> struggle against all my life. Rather, by grace God grants me the
> righteousness of Christ to free me forever from judgment.

The Heidelberg Catechism goes on to explicate what believing in the
Holy Spirit means, and turns now to the church as its next subject
matter in a rather characteristic way, providing us again with yet
another of its "gems". Despite being known and praised (and also
sometimes criticized) as one of the most personal confessions of
faith, we would completely misinterpret the Heidelberg Catechism's
understanding of the church if we develop it from an individualistic
perspective. Quite the opposite is true: if we follow the sequence set
by the Heidelberg Catechism, the individual church member *concludes* the list of what we believe concerning the church. Subject of the
answer here is not the individual Christian, choosing to be a member
of this or that church, or a group of Christian believers forming a
church; the subject is the *Son of God* through his Spirit and Word.
The origin, preservation, and aim of the church all lay outside of the
church and are the work of its head, Christ, in what he did, is doing,
and will do. Thus the "sole comfort" of belonging to God pertains to
the communion of God just as it does to the individual believer. In
fact, the individual believer cannot be understood apart from God's
chosen community of which she is, and will remain, a member. The
Heidelberg Catechism does not know of a private, individualistic
Christianity; to be a Christian means to be a member of the Christian
church. (It may be helpful to recall at this point, that the Heidelberg
Catechism presupposes a church context and was written primarily
not for private use, but for the church's preaching, teaching, liturgy,
and so on.) The Spirit has been given to each believer personally
(cf. question 53), but not individualistically (Allen Verhey). Thus,
the Spirit binds the believer to the church, the community chosen
for eternal life, united in true faith. The doctrine of election, of God
choosing human beings for salvation and serving God's intention for
the world, which has been of particular importance for the Reformed
tradition, is discussed here accordingly as a *communal* election and
not an individual one. God gathers, protects and preserves human
beings from the *entire human race* – a still noteworthy specification
for all contexts, and an especially essential one for the Confession of

Belhar (mentioned above in chapter 1). Another specification the Heidelberg Catechism provides us with in this description of the church carries great theological weight: "from the beginning of the world to its end" translates into the true ecumenical character of the church in every time and every place, and it also includes Israel as the people of God, since God will never forsake God's covenant. As members of Christ's church, we thus find ourselves in a fellowship not only with the contemporaries in our own particular church, but with all Christians of all times and places; a fellowship that is truly *catholic,* in the sense of "universal", because Christ is the universal head of it, and that is truly *holy,* because Christ is holy and we are engrafted into him through the Holy Spirit. How do we live as "holy people" who share in Christ and all his treasures and gifts; how do we live as the *communion of saints?* The communion of saints, of those people who have been gathered into the church and made holy – and the passive voice is of critical importance here –, is essentially a diaconal fellowship, where all participate actively in serving and enriching each other, for the mutual benefit of all. Just as Christ shares his benefits with the individual believer and the communion of the saints, the church as a whole and each of its members is called not to boast of their gifts, spiritual or other, or else to regard them as their possession, but to share them in gratitude and joy. The gift contains a task; and we may hear this understanding echoed in another confession of faith, the Theological Declaration of Barmen from 1934, when it states most memorably in its Second Thesis: "As Jesus Christ is God's assurance of the forgiveness of all our sins, so in the same way and with the same seriousness is he also God's mighty claim upon our whole life. Through him befalls us a joyful deliverance from the godless fetters of this world for a free, grateful service to his creatures." Recalling the concluding words of question 1, it becomes clear, too, that this service cannot be understood as means to any form of works righteousness, but is indeed based on the work of the Holy Spirit.

From this we may understand better why the forgiveness of sins (question 56), which has been dealt with several times before, has indeed its place in this discussion of the church: those "saints" that have been gathered together in God's communion are holy not because they live holy and righteous lives, but because *God* has granted them *Christ's* righteousness. The church is the communion of saints as "the church of pardoned sinners", to quote the Theological Declaration of Barmen once more; therefore the church stands in solidarity *with* all children of God, not above or apart from them. The comfort of belonging to God, then, is interpreted in the context of the doctrine of the church as *always* belonging to God's church, despite our continuing sinfulness, and as being freed from judgment *forever,* and this leads the believer immediately into a life of gratitude and joy.

Lord's Day 22 (57–58): Resurrection and Life Everlasting

> Q. 57 How does "the resurrection of the body" comfort you?
> A. Not only will my soul be taken immediately after this life to Christ its head, but also my very flesh will be raised by the power of Christ, reunited with my soul, and made like Christ's glorious body.
>
> Q. 58 How does the article concerning "life everlasting" comfort you?
> A. Even as I already now experience in my heart the beginning of eternal joy, so after this life I will have perfect blessedness such as no eye has seen, no ear has heard, no human heart has ever imagined: a blessedness in which to praise God forever.

As we have noted above, the Heidelberg Catechism uses the term "comfort" rather sparsely, though it remains of indisputable significance for its theological perspective; after the two introductory question, we encounter this term only in questions 52 (the comfort of the return of Christ), 53 (the Holy Spirit as Comforter), and now here in questions 57 and 58. Maybe somewhat startling for contemporary Christians, the Heidelberg Catechism connects comfort with the work of the Holy Spirit, and with Christ's work as it pertains to our future, or rather: to *Christ's future* with us. Our comfort is that we have been given a hope that reaches beyond the limit of our own life, a hope that lies outside of ourselves, a hope not *for* something but *in* someone, Christ. The church of the pardoned sinners is the church of hope, living in the "already and not yet", looking backwards to the incarnation, crucifixion, resurrection and looking forward to meet its Head and Judge, who is at the same time the pledge of the believer's own resurrection (see questions 45 and 49). In this resurrection, the unit of body and soul of the believer, the whole mortal person, is restored by his faithful Savior, to whom he already belongs with body and soul in past, present and future – not even death can put an end to our belonging to God, since death is not eternal, but God's loving grace is (Eberhard Busch). Those who as finite human beings have no future beyond death are given a future in Christ; eternal life means being finally taken home to the One we already belong to. That is the comfort the Heidelberg Catechism sees at the heart of the Gospel.

And this comfort is at work *already* in the believer's heart as the beginning of eternal joy; here and now the believer is consoled and encouraged, experiencing the beginnings of blessedness. What is this blessedness like? The Heidelberg Catechism is very concrete and specific in its answer, which concurs with other central catechisms of the Reformed tradition (such as the Westminster and Calvin's Genevan, for example). The perfect blessedness of human beings, their ultimate goal and chief end, consists in *praising God forever* (see also question 6); maybe a somewhat eccentric thought for our time, which is so preoccupied with self-fulfillment, but certainly characteristically Reformed. Praising God, though, is not an activity deferred to our "heavenly life", but a concrete life-style and attitude with immediate consequences for all our actions, since we already now – by the work of the Holy Spirit – experience the beginnings of eternal joy, which lead us directly into a life of gratitude and service (see questions 86 and 122, for example). In other words, Christians await the One to come, who is their Head and whose members they are already today.

Lord's Day 23 & 24 (59–64): Righteousness and Good Works

Q. 59 What good does it do you, however, to believe all this?
A. In Christ I am righteous before God and heir to life everlasting.

Q. 60 How are you righteous before God?
A. Only by true faith in Jesus Christ. Even though my conscience accuses me of having grievously sinned against all God's commandments, of never having kept any of them, and of still being inclined toward all evil, nevertheless, without any merit of my own, out of sheer grace, God grants and credits to me the perfect satisfaction, righteousness, and holiness of Christ, as if I had never sinned nor been a sinner, and as if I had been as perfectly obedient as Christ was obedient for me. All I need to do is accept this gift with a believing heart.

Q. 61 Why do you say that through faith alone you are righteous?
A. Not because I please God by the worthiness of my faith. It is because only Christ's satisfaction, righteousness, and holiness make me righteous before God, and because I can accept this righteousness and make it mine in no other way than through faith.

Q. 62 Why can't our good works be our righteousness before God, or at least a part of our righteousness?
A. Because the righteousness which can pass God's judgment must be entirely perfect and must in every way measure up to the divine law. But even our best works in this life are imperfect and stained with sin.

Q. 63 How can our good works be said to merit nothing when God promises to reward them in this life and the next?
A. This reward is not earned; it is a gift of grace.

Q. 64 But doesn't this teaching make people indifferent and wicked?
A. No. It is impossible for those grafted into Christ through true faith not to produce fruits of gratitude.

With question 58, the Heidelberg Catechism has concluded its exposition of the Apostles' Creed, but it does add six more questions before turning to the next subject. And although these six question do not actually add anything materially new to what has been said before, they provide us with a fine summary not only of the central message of the Apostles' Creed as understood by the authors of the Heidelberg Catechism, but also of the "most precious discoveries of the Reformation" (Fred Klooster). If you want to know what theological issues and pastoral concerns lay at the heart of the Reformation, a look at questions 59 through 64 would provide you with an excellent synopsis of its main insights.

Questions 59 starts this section off with a rather peculiar question, asked not by the catechumen, the student, but – remarkably so – by the teacher, the catechist: "What good does it do you to believe all this"? There is a deep pastoral, spiritual concern discernable in this question. Knowing and believing the promises of the gospel as they are summarized in the Apostles' Creed is not an abstract, theoretical practice, but it does the believer good; in Christ and through true faith I am righteous before God – this is what the Reformation had emphasized over and over again; this is what the Heidelberg Catechism understands as the sole comfort of the believer. The exposition of the Apostles' Creed is framed by two questions helping us to understand the role of faith in the life of the believer. Question 22 asks what a Christian *must* believe: the promise of the gospel that we belong to God; and question 59 asks what *good it does us* to believe all this: in Christ we are righteous before God (one of the shortest answers of the whole catechism). In that sense, question 59 could be understand as a summary not only of the Apostles' Creed, but of the entire Christian faith – as understood at the time of the late Reformation age. And with the answer to question 60, which is one of the longest ones of the whole catechism, we encounter another, more detailed summary, an expression of "the core of Reformed faith" (Hendrikus Berkhoff). Again, we find the already mentioned watchwords of the Reformation: Sola Gratia, Sola Fide, Solus Christus (by grace alone, by faith alone, Christ alone), in another effort to explain the strange logic of grace once more, the "joyous exchange", without adding new material or thoughts. The Heidelberg Catechism comes back over and again to this central issue from all other considerations, because none of them can be understood rightly if they are not related to Christ as our righteousness. Answer 60 begins by stating again that human misery, sin, actually pervades everything we are and do; there is nothing in us and our works that would be righteous and meritory, and our conscience tells us so. Yet, and this is the "big yet of the gospel", the strange logic of grace, God grants and credits to us *out of sheer grace* the satisfaction, righteousness, and holiness of Christ; this is the pivotal element here. We are, to quote a much-cited formula going back to Martin Luther, *simul iustus et peccator* (simultaneously righteous and sinner). And in true faith, in which we accept this and rely on God alone, we receive Christ's righteousness as a gift. As question 61 makes clear: it is not our faith that makes us righteous before God, faith is not a "good work"; we are made righteous by the object and content of our faith. Faith itself, as sure knowledge and wholehearted trust, is the product of the activity of the Holy Spirit in us (see questions 21 and 65), and could therefore never be mistaken as our own work. In other words, *in faith* we can be sure, comforted, and encouraged, not *because of faith*. In faith, we understand that we neither can nor have to justify ourselves, *and* that in Christ, we are already justified. Accepting this with a believing heart means absolute confidence and trust in God, and that is true faith.

Good works, however, are nevertheless neither obsolete nor irrelevant, even though they are always stained by sin, only a beginning of our obedience (question 114), and all rewards we earn in this life and later (question 63) are gifts of grace. In question 64, we hear the voices of people seriously and piously contemplating this justification by grace through faith alone and its consequences: does this teaching not lead people to become indifferent and wicked? Why should we do good works at all, if they neither count for our justification nor are actually good? Why does the Bible speak of our rewards, if there is no merit from our part? Those were actual questions asked by Roman Catholic opponents of this Reformation teaching, signifying one essential controversy between the Church of Rome and Protestant churches up until today. What we touch upon here is, also, the starting point for all Christian ethics, and an immensely practical and also inevitable challenge for the Christian church in every time and place: how do we live as those belonging to God? As question 64 notes, all believers have been grafted into Christ (which is the work of the Holy Spirit, see question 80), have been made right with God *and* neighbors, have been freed *from* the pressure to try and justify themselves and *for* a life in solidarity, and as a result of this, good works are the thankful response of the justified believer as well as of the church of pardoned sinners. Not producing good fruits of gratitude is thus an "impossible possibility" (Fred Klooster) for those engrafted into Christ.

Any ethics developed from this point of view can only be understood principally as an "ethic of gratitude", and not as an ethic of fear, reason, or blind obedience. Part III will demonstrate this ethic of gratitude in detail.

The Holy Sacraments

Lord's Day 25 (65–68): Signs and Seals

Q. 65 It is through faith alone that we share in Christ and all his benefits: where then does that faith come from?
A. The Holy Spirit produces it in our hearts by the preaching of the holy gospel, and confirms it by the use of the holy sacraments.

Q. 66 What are sacraments?
A. Sacraments are visible, holy signs and seals. They were instituted by God so that by our use of them he might make us understand more clearly the promise of the gospel, and seal that promise. And this is God's gospel promise: to grant us forgiveness of sins and eternal life by grace because of Christ's one sacrifice accomplished on the cross.

Q. 67 Are both the word and the sacraments then intended to focus our faith on the sacrifice of Jesus Christ on the cross as the only ground of our salvation?
A. Yes! In the gospel the Holy Spirit teaches us and by the holy sacraments confirms that our entire salvation rests on Christ's one sacrifice for us on the cross.

Q. 68 How many sacraments did Christ institute in the New Testament?
A. Two: holy baptism and the holy supper.

With questions 65 to 68 we move closer to the central issues that lead
to controversies, disputes, and even actual persecution not only in
Heidelberg, but all over Europe in the 16th century, and that provided
the actual occasion for drafting the Heidelberg Catechism. As we
may remember, the debate on the true and faithful understanding
of the sacraments, especially the Lord's Supper, caused a split not
only between the Protestant and Roman Catholic sides, but also
within the Protestant camp. We may also recall, how Frederick III
was convinced that this issue in particular had to be resolved in
order to promote the true worship of God. For that reason, it does
not come as a surprise that roughly a fifth of the Heidelberg Catechism (measured by the word count) is devoted to this subject in
rather elaborate and lengthy answers. This certainly was a section of
the catechism that called for meticulous and diligent considerations
and formulations, for theological, pastoral, and also political reasons.
The concentration and focus on the doctrine of sacraments, which
was also part of the classical material of catechesis throughout the
centuries, led to a rather unexpected deficiency of the Heidelberg
Catechism: even though the catechism puts great stress on the fact
that the Holy Spirit creates true faith in our hearts by the preaching
of the gospel, that the Spirit teaches us the Gospel promise, that
both – Word and Sacrament – intend to focus our faith on Christ, we
nowhere in the Heidelberg Catechism find a closer consideration of
the creation of true faith by preaching or teaching, or a doctrine of
the Word in general. Nevertheless, the Heidelberg Catechism does
not separate preaching and the sacraments from each other, just the
opposite, both are instruments of the Holy Spirit in *creating* faith in
us (through the proclamation) and *confirming* faith in us (in the use
of the sacraments). The very same grace of God is mediated through
the preaching of the Word as through the use of the sacraments; there
is no special or different grace in the Lord's Supper and baptism, and
thus no reason to value sacraments differently from preaching. There
is but one justifying faith, yet two interdependent actions of the Holy
Spirit in creating and confirming, as well as two interdependent acts
of the church in preaching and sacraments, as question 65 points
out in order to explain the connection between the doctrine of faith
and the sacraments. The individual believers, as well as the commu-

nion of saints, are simultaneously active and passive here, acting and receiving, subject and object – all by the power of the Holy Spirit; it is God, who makes these human acts effective.

Only in this way can we understand the Heidelberg Catechism's description of the sacraments as "signs and seals" correctly. The expression "signs" does not refer to an empty, mere sign as if there was nothing more than what we see; they are visible, earthly signs tied by God to an act of God and in that sense, they only *become* signs through the work of the Holy Spirit. Sacraments could therefore also be understood as "eventful witnesses to God's righteous action in Jesus Christ" (Karl Barth). Consequently, not only the *elements* (bread and wine in the Lord's Supper, water in the baptism) are understood here as signs, but more so the *use* of the elements (washing with water and nourishing through a meal of bread and wine) is the sign for the action of God, as we will see later in the more detailed discussion of baptism and the Lord's Supper. This understanding is clarified throughout the entire section on sacraments in the Heidelberg Catechism by the recurring use of the significant expression "as surely as" … "so surely/certainly/truly" (which the Heidelberg Catechism learned from Calvin and Augustine). That is to say, *as surely as we are washed by the water and nourished by bread and wine, so surely* we are washed with Christ's Blood and Spirit and nourished for eternal life. Hence, sacraments are understood as auxiliary means and visual aids applied by the Holy Spirit, visible signs of an invisible grace (Augustine), by which we understand more clearly what God promises us in the Holy Gospel, thus confirming and sealing this promise of forgiveness of sins and eternal life out of sheer grace.

Proclamation and sacraments are both intimately and indissolubly related to the cross in a twofold way: they not only focus our faith on this very sacrifice of Christ, but they also mediate the gifts of grace, gained for us by Christ's sacrifice on the cross (question 67). According to the Heidelberg Catechism, neither preaching nor the sacraments can be understood apart from the cross, or else they would no longer proclaim and confirm God's gospel promise. What, then, differentiates preaching from the sacraments? Two main aspects need to be mentioned here: 1. It is through preaching that the Holy Spirit creates true faith – without preaching there would be no faith;

in the sacraments, this faith is confirmed and sealed. Hence, the sacraments *presuppose* faith and do not cause it *ex opera operato* ("from the work having worked"). 2. Preaching refers us more to the content of God's promise, that is, *what* God does for and with us, while the sacraments refer us to the carrying out of God's promise, *that* God *does* this to us and with us (Eberhard Busch). With these two aspects in mind, we clearly see that, even though a specific unit on preaching is absent in the Heidelberg Catechism, the actual appreciation of the central role of preaching in creating true faith is by no means ignored in this catechism; on the contrary, we will encounter proclamation again in quite a number of important questions.

But back to the issue of sacraments; so far, the Heidelberg Catechism has discussed them in general without identifying them in particular. In question 68 now, the Heidelberg Catechism names the two sacraments the Protestant churches recognize as biblical, that means, as being instituted by Christ: Holy Baptism and the Holy Supper. For most Protestants, this answer may seem rather self-evident, even obsolete, because they are already accustomed to this number, and may not even know that it varies in different denominations. For 16th century believers, though, this question was not that evident altogether: the Roman Catholic church, as declared by the Council of Trent (1545–1563), recognized seven sacraments (baptism, confirmation, holy Eucharist, penance, anointing of the sick, holy orders, and matrimony), while most Protestant churches limited the number of sacraments to the above mentioned two (sometimes, though, adding penance as a third), because they found only these two warranted by New Testament writings as being instituted by Christ. Even in the determination of the number of sacraments, therefore, the two Protestant principles of "Christ alone" and "by Scripture alone" play a decisive role for the Heidelberg Catechism.

Lord's Day 26 & 27 (69–74): Holy Baptism

Q. 69 How does baptism remind and assure you that Christ's one sacrifice on the cross benefits you personally?
A. In this way: Christ instituted this outward washing and with it promised that, as surely as water washes away the dirt from the

body, so certainly his blood and his Spirit wash away my soul's impurity, that is, all my sins.

Q. 70 What does it mean to be washed with Christ's blood and Spirit?
A. To be washed with Christ's blood means that God, by grace, has forgiven our sins because of Christ's blood poured out for us in his sacrifice on the cross. To be washed with Christ's Spirit means that the Holy Spirit has renewed and sanctified us to be members of Christ, so that more and more we become dead to sin and live holy and blameless lives.

Q. 71. Where does Christ promise that we are washed with his blood and Spirit as surely as we are washed with the water of baptism?
A. In the institution of baptism, where he says: "Go therefore and make disciples of all nations, baptizing them in the name of the Father and of the Son and of the Holy Spirit." "The one who believes and is baptized will be saved; but the one who does not believe will be condemned." This promise is repeated when Scripture calls baptism "the water of rebirth" and the washing away of sins.

Q. 72 Does this outward washing with water itself wash away sins?
A. No, only Jesus Christ's blood and the Holy Spirit cleanse us from all sins.

Q. 73 Why then does the Holy Spirit call baptism the water of rebirth and the washing away of sins?
A. God has good reason for these words. To begin with, God wants to teach us that the blood and Spirit of Christ take away our sins just as water removes dirt from the body. But more important, God wants to assure us, by this divine pledge and sign, that we are as truly washed of our sins spiritually as our bodies are washed with water physically.

Q. 74 Should infants also be baptized?
A. Yes. Infants as well as adults are included in God's covenant and people, and they, no less than adults, are promised deliverance from sin through Christ's blood and the Holy Spirit who produces faith.

Therefore, by baptism, the sign of the covenant, they too should be incorporated into the Christian church and distinguished from the children of unbelievers. This was done in the Old Testament by circumcision, which was replaced in the New Testament by baptism.

The formulation of question 69 sets the tone for the next five questions, and thus for the discussion of baptism in general, in offering three phrases that form a theological and, at the same time, pastoral framework. These phrases are: "remind and assure", "Christ's one sacrifice on the cross", and "benefit you personally", and they are more than accurate and adequate theological terms, more than doctrinally orthodox watchwords; they are an effort to interpret the meaning of Good Friday for each believer individually. Note that the Heidelberg Catechism does not simply ask for a definition of what baptism is in itself! In line with its incessant emphasis on the believer's comfort, the catechism instead enquires how baptism *reminds and assures us,* to begin with the first phrase. "Reminds" and "assures" are two different expressions for what the Heidelberg Catechism before called "signs and seals": sacraments as signs remind us and as seals assure as. In other words, they describe the function of sacraments, of what they are *doing;* they remind and assure the believer of what Christ has done for us, with us, and in us. Accordingly, baptism points us not only to Christ's *one sacrifice on the cross* where he gained righteousness for us, but also affirms for us that we *benefit personally* from this sacrifice. Baptism has to do with me and Christ in the most personal, intimate relationship conceivable, a true union with Christ that is not produced through baptism, but which is witnessed to in baptism. The act of baptism itself does not effect anything in itself (question 72); the Holy Spirit employs this earthly sign of outward washing, of cleansing with water, pointing us towards God's action in Christ. Or as question 69 puts it: Christ promises us that *as surely* as the water cleanses the body, *so certainly* Christ's blood and Spirit cleanse us from all our sins. And question 73 adds, that God's "assurance" in baptism as the water of rebirth and washing away of sin is even of more importance than God's "teaching" in this act. Not because God's teaching was less important in itself; the Heidelberg Catechism rather wants to emphasize again that God's teaching has a certain aim: God wants to assure and comfort us; the true faith that is created in us by the work of the Holy Spirit is simultaneously a sure knowledge and wholehearted trust (question 21).

Each of the questions in this section employs the concept of a washing with Christ's Blood and Spirit; maybe a rather disconcerting concept for contemporary believers. The Heidelberg Catechism, though, uses this expression to point us towards Christ's priestly and kingly office and our benefits from those, as we have already noted above under question 1. Question 79, now, takes up these two terms and asks what this twofold washing of baptism means for us, or, to put it differently: what it means to be a Christian (in that sense, question 79 is yet another attempt to respond to question 32: but why are you called a Christian?). It is through the *acts of God* in crucifixion and resurrection that we already entered into the fellowship with Jesus Christ, into the fellowship of his death and resurrection. In baptism we are told that we *are* Christians, that because of Christ's once and for all sacrifice, we can be certain of our faith and the forgiveness of our sins once and for all: Christ died and rose again for us also! (Karl Barth). Baptism is more than proclamation; it also is a divine pledge and witnesses to us that nobody is born a Christian or has to make himself or herself Christian; instead, we are made Christians by Christ through the Holy Spirit.

Question 79 does not leave it at the justification aspect of baptism (the washing with Christ's blood), but adds, in a distinctively Reformed way, a second perspective: through the washing with the Spirit, we are renewed and sanctified to be members of Christ, already here and now. We are brought into a right relationship with God by God, and this means, as we have seen before, that we are not only declared righteous by God, but that the Holy Spirit makes us righteous so that we are enabled to make a small beginning in living holy and blameless lives. Not that we ever leave sin behind us completely! We have seen how seriously the catechism takes the reality and power of sin over our lives (for example in question 60), and yet it also acknowledges the work of the Holy Spirit in the life of Christians. This life-changing, life-renewing power of the Holy Spirit, this rebirth of the believer, which is attested to in baptism, pertains to the entire life of the Christian, and not only the religious part of it.

For that reason, baptism could be understood as the foundation of all Christian ethics; part III will elaborate this perspective in detail. We can already note at this point, however, that baptism (and also the Lord's Supper) has direct consequences on how we lead our lives in its entirety as those belonging to God, engrafted in Christ, and washed with the Spirit. The grace of God signed and sealed in baptism is no cheap grace; the comfort of belonging to God is no cheap comfort, but entails a "mighty claim upon our whole life" (Barmen Theological Declaration).

The last question of this section deals with the subject of baptizing infants in vehemently defending this praxis. Facing the challenges of the radical Reformation movement, called the Anabaptists ("baptizing again"), which rejected infant baptisms and called for a believer's baptism, the authors of the Heidelberg Catechism vindicated infant baptism just as strongly as all major Reformation camps and the Roman Catholic church. With reference to the Holy Spirit, the producer of faith, the Heidelberg Catechism understands baptism in this question as a *covenant sign* which infants should also receive, even though they may show no sign of faith yet, and despite the fact that most of what the Heidelberg Catechism has to say about baptism seems to presuppose the faith of the baptized.

Lord's Day 28–30 (75–82): The Holy Supper of Jesus Christ

Q. 75 How does the holy supper remind and assure you that you share in Christ's one sacrifice on the cross and in all his benefits? A. In this way: Christ has commanded me and all believers to eat this broken bread and to drink this cup in remembrance of him. With this command come these promises: First, as surely as I see with my eyes the bread of the Lord broken for me and the cup shared with me, so surely his body was offered and broken for me and his blood poured out for me on the cross. Second, as surely as I receive from the hand of the one who serves, and taste with my mouth the bread and cup of the Lord, given me as sure signs of Christ's body and blood, so surely he nourishes and refreshes my soul for eternal life with his crucified body and poured-out blood.

Q. 76 What does it mean to eat the crucified body of Christ and to drink his poured-out blood?

A. It means to accept with a believing heart the entire suffering and death of Christ and thereby to receive forgiveness of sins and eternal life. But it means more. Through the Holy Spirit, who lives both in Christ and in us, we are united more and more to Christ's blessed body. And so, although he is in heaven and we are on earth, we are flesh of his flesh and bone of his bone. And we forever live on and are governed by one Spirit, as the members of our body are by one soul.

Q. 77 Where does Christ promise to nourish and refresh believers with his body and blood as surely as they eat this broken bread and drink this cup?

A. In the institution of the Lord's Supper: "The Lord Jesus, on the night when he was betrayed, took a loaf of bread, and when he had given thanks, he broke it and said, 'This is my body that is [broken][2] for you.' In the same way he took the cup also, after supper, saying, 'This cup is the new covenant in my blood; do this, as often as you drink it, in remembrance of me.' For as often as you eat this bread and drink the cup, you proclaim the Lord's death until he comes." This promise is repeated by Paul in these words: "The cup of blessing that we bless, is it not a sharing in the blood of Christ? The bread that we break, is it not a sharing in the body of Christ? Because there is one bread, we who are many are one body, for we all partake of the one bread."

Q. 78 Do the bread and wine become the real body and blood of Christ?

A. No. Just as the water of baptism is not changed into Christ's blood and does not itself wash away sins but is simply a divine sign and assurance of these things, so too the holy bread of the Lord's Supper does not become the actual body of Christ, even though it is called the body of Christ in keeping with the nature and language of sacraments.

---

2   The word "broken" does not appear in the NRSV text, but it was present in the original German of the Heidelberg Catechism.

Q. 79 Why then does Christ call the bread his body and the cup his blood, or the new covenant in his blood, and Paul use the words, a participation in Christ's body and blood?

A. Christ has good reason for these words. He wants to teach us that just as bread and wine nourish the temporal life, so too his crucified body and poured-out blood are the true food and drink of our souls for eternal life. But more important, he wants to assure us, by this visible sign and pledge, that we, through the Holy Spirit's work, share in his true body and blood as surely as our mouths receive these holy signs in his remembrance, and that all of his suffering and obedience are as definitely ours as if we personally had suffered and made satisfaction for our sins.

Q. 80 How does the Lord's Supper differ from the Roman Catholic Mass?

A. The Lord's Supper declares to us that all our sins are completely forgiven through the one sacrifice of Jesus Christ, which he himself accomplished on the cross once for all. It also declares to us that the Holy Spirit grafts us into Christ, who with his true body is now in heaven at the right hand of the Father where he wants us to worship him. But the Mass teaches that the living and the dead do not have their sins forgiven through the suffering of Christ unless Christ is still offered for them daily by the priests. It also teaches that Christ is bodily present under the form of bread and wine where Christ is therefore to be worshiped. Thus the Mass is basically nothing but a denial of the one sacrifice and suffering of Jesus Christ and a condemnable idolatry.[3]

---

3   Some Reformed and Presbyterian Churches have added varying comments to question 80; three of them are cited here by way of an example:
Presbyterian Church (USA): Question and Answer 80 reflects the polemical debates of the Reformation and was added in the second German edition of 1563. The second and fourth sentences of the Answer, as well as the concluding phrase, were added in the third German edition of 1563. After the fourth sentence, the third German and Latin texts have a note to the section on consecration in the Canon of the Mass.
As detailed in the preface to The Book of Confessions, these condemnations and characterizations of the Catholic Church are not the position of the Presbyte-

Q. 81 Who should come to the Lord's table?
A. Those who are displeased with themselves because of their sins, but who nevertheless trust that their sins are pardoned and that their remaining weakness is covered by the suffering and death of Christ, and who also desire more and more to strengthen their faith and to lead a better life. Hypocrites and those who are unrepentant, however, eat and drink judgment on themselves.

Q. 82 Should those be admitted to the Lord's Supper who show by what they profess and how they live that they are unbelieving and ungodly?
A. No, that would dishonor God's covenant and bring down God's wrath upon the entire congregation. Therefore, according to the instruction of Christ and his apostles, the Christian church is duty-bound to exclude such people, by the official use of the keys of the kingdom, until they reform their lives.

With the historical and theological background in mind, it does not surprise to see how the Heidelberg Catechism develops the doctrine

---

rian Church (U.S.A.) and are not applicable to current relationships between the Presbyterian Church (U.S.A.) and the Catholic Church.
Christian Reformed Church in North America: Q&A 80 was altogether absent from the first edition of the catechism but was present in a shorter form in the second edition. The translation here given is of the expanded text of the third edition. In response to a mandate from Synod 1998, the Christian Reformed Church's Interchurch Relations Committee conducted a study of Q&A 80 and the Roman Catholic Mass. Based on this study, Synod 2004 declared that "Q&A 80 can no longer be held in its current form as part of our confession." Synod 2006 directed that Q&A 80 remain in the CRC's text of the Heidelberg Catechism but that the last three paragraphs be placed in brackets to indicate that they do not accurately reflect the official teaching and practice of today's Roman Catholic Church and are no longer confessionally binding on members of the CRC.
Reformed Church in America: Q&A 80 was altogether absent from the first edition of the catechism but was present in a shorter form in the second edition. The translation here given is of the expanded text of the third edition. The Reformed Church in America retains the original full text, choosing to recognize that the catechism was written within a historical context which may not accurately describe the Roman Catholic Church's current stance.

of the Lord's Supper in even greater detail and with more complex answers than the doctrine of baptism. A second indication of how seriously the authors took this section, how essential they deemed a theological clarification of this highly controversial issue, is the great number of biblical reference texts the catechism provides in this section. Frederick later stated confidently in his defense before the Emperor Maximilian II: "This catechism has on its pages such abundant proof from Holy Scripture that it will remain unrefuted by men and will also remain my irrefutable belief." This was certainly also the conviction of the committee with respect to the Heidelberg Catechism in general, and this critical part in particular.

Questions 75 through 79 are structured in parallel to questions 69–73; with questions 74 and 80 as rather contextual add-ons. For that reason, we find in this lengthy passage many elements, we have already encountered before in the discussion of the doctrine of baptism: the understanding of the function of the Lord's Supper as "reminding and assuring"; the reference to Christ's one sacrifice on the cross and its benefits for us; the use of the structuring element "as surely … so surely"; the work of the Holy Spirit in uniting us "more and more" to Christ; the aspect of teaching and, "more important", the assurance aspect of the Lord's Supper; the understanding that the elements are not in themselves to be understood as the signs, but their use in nourishing and refreshing believers; the conviction that participation in the Lord's Supper is both gift and claim. Of course, these parallels are to be expected since they refer to the general doctrine of sacraments in the Heidelberg Catechism, and develop from the catechism's teaching that neither baptism nor the Lord's Supper impart any form of special grace, but are related to the one true faith and God's gift of grace. In that sense, the Lord's Supper is another assurance and pledge of the comfort the Holy Spirit is giving to each believer, another confirmation of the faith created in her or him. We will therefore focus our deliberations on three issues of particular importance: a) the understanding of Christ's body and blood, and what the Lord's Supper adds as means of grace; b) the relation of the Lord's Supper, Christian life and discipline; and, finally, c) the special case of question 80.

a) The starting point for any deliberation on the Lord's Supper is the fact that Jesus Christi in the Holy Spirit is its *acting subject* in multiple ways. To begin with, the Lord's Supper is not a human invention, nor merely a church practice, but commanded and instituted by Christ, and it remains just this in every respect, the *Lord's* Supper. It's the Lord whose promises come with this command and institution, and it is the Lord to whom we are truly, personally united with and bound to, sharing in his true body and blood, becoming flesh of his flesh, bone of his bone, being engrafted in him. The Lord establishes, by the accompanying use of the signs in breaking the bread and sharing the cup, the relation between what happens in the congregation at the Lord's Table and his own once-and-for-all sacrifice on the cross, and by this, we truly share in Christ's benefits. The present Lord, present spiritually and not physically in the elements of bread and wine, gives himself to the believers, feeds them for eternal life, and nourishes them on their way. As baptism is considered the sacrament of beginning and therefore administered but once, so the Lord's Supper is the sacrament of sustaining, and is administered on a regular basis to strengthen and encourage the faith of the believers again and again, so that believers may live through and with him. As baptism teaches and assures us of how our faith and being Christian is founded objectively in Christ, so the Lord's Supper teaches and assures us of how our faith and being Christian is being preserved objectively by Christ. In the Lord's Supper, thus, we encounter a concrete and visual aid to what question 54 stated on Christ as the Head of the church, in that it is the Lord who "gathers, protects, and preserves for himself a community chosen for eternal life and united in true faith", and the believer tastes, sees, hears, and is assured of the promise that "of this community I am and always will be a living member". Not of his or her own strength, though! Christ is the subject of the Lord's Supper also in that it is him who gives us the strength to persevere, who renews our faith again and again, and who covers our remaining weakness.

b) If we consider question 80 as an insertion, the section of questions 75 through 85 (including the questions on the office of keys) is structured by two sets of five articles each: whereas questions 74 through 79 deal with the grace of Christ as it is witnessed to us in the Lord's Supper, questions 81 through 85 deal with our reaction and answer to this grace. This reaction and answer is best described as

"giving thanks" for God's grace, and Christian life is thus best understood as a *Eucharistic life* in the original sense of the term, keeping in
mind that the Greek noun *eucharistia* actually means "thanksgiving".
Being brought into communion with Christ by the Holy Spirit, the
community of Christ is engrafted into Christ and as such shares in
his obedience. That means that all members of this community of
Christ, governed and sanctified by the one Spirit, communally and
individually, desire to strengthen their own faith *and* lead a better life,
a Eucharistic life. What constitutes this Eucharistic life? First of all,
it is the life of pardoned sinners who are displeased with themselves,
but nevertheless trust in the forgiveness of their sins and give thanks
for it. It is not a life without sin, because nobody can live up perfectly
to God's law (question 4), and all are sinners. Eucharistic life is not
the life of morally or ethically superior people, but the life of those
who know themselves as weak people, yet strive to lead a better life.
Those who are "hypocrites and unrepentant", either because they do
not admit their sins or trust in themselves instead of God, who do
not understand themselves to be in need of God's grace, "eat and
drink judgment on themselves" (question 81). This harsh formulation, quoted from 1 Cor 11:29, has had a quite traumatic influence on
generations of Reformed Christians, who developed something of a
reluctance and even dread to participate in the Lord's Supper from
sheer fear of belonging to those "unworthy people" who eat and drink
judgment on themselves. The Heidelberg Catechism, though, was not
aiming at scaring believers away from the Lord's Table, but just the
opposite; it aimed at reminding the believers, in accordance with Paul,
of the significance of the Lord's Supper as the source of all Eucharistic
life, of the costly gift and comfort of God's grace. Those who deny their
absolute dependence on this gift and comfort of God's grace in teaching, worshipping, and living, those who deny with words or acts God's
claim on their whole life, dishonor not only God's covenant, but also
endanger the whole congregation. The believers' conduct of life and
their behavior matters, and the communion of saints, communally
and individually, is held responsible for living a Eucharistic life. We
will get back to this understanding in discussing the office of the keys.

c) Question 80 now constitutes to some extent a special case,
not only because its rather antagonistic tone presents an obvious

breach of style with the conciliatory and irenic attitude of the rest of the catechism, but also because this question was added in later editions of the Heidelberg Catechism, and was absent from the first edition (January 1563). It was on the behest of Frederick III that this question was inserted, a shorter version already into the second edition (March 1563), and the full version into the third edition (April 1563). What we encounter here in its negative statements is a reaction to the Counter-Reformation, Roman Catholic condemnations of Protestants positions on the Lord's Supper as formulated in the so-called "anathemas" of the Council of Trent (1545–1563). It is a rather contextual supplement, inserted by an enraged Elector Palatinate, who had probably just recently learned about the latest Anti-Protestant condemnations of the 22nd session that closed a few months ago. Two aspects of this "counter-counter-condemnation" remain controversial and debated until today, that is, whether this description of the mass actually reflects Roman Catholic teaching on mass, and whether contemporary churches agree with condemning mass as idolatry. For that reason, several churches have added comments to this particular question (see footnote to question 80). What should not be overlooked, though, is that question 80 does not only formulate negative statements against Roman Catholic teaching, but also states positively what it sees at the heart of the doctrine of the Lord's Supper, what is signified to and sealed by breaking the bread and sharing the cup: the forgiveness of sins through Christ's one sacrifice, once and for all, and our being engrafted into Christ by the Holy Spirit.

Lord's Day 31 (83–85): Office of the Keys: Preaching the Gospel and Christian Discipline

Q. 83 What are the keys of the kingdom?
A. The preaching of the holy gospel and Christian discipline toward repentance. Both of them open the kingdom of heaven to believers and close it to unbelievers.

Q. 84 How does preaching the holy gospel open and close the kingdom of heaven?

A. According to the command of Christ, the kingdom of heaven is opened by proclaiming and publicly declaring to all believers, each and every one, that, as often as they accept the gospel promise in true faith, God, because of Christ's merit, truly forgives all their sins. The kingdom of heaven is closed, however, by proclaiming and publicly declaring to unbelievers and hypocrites that, as long as they do not repent, the wrath of God and eternal condemnation rest on them. God's judgment, both in this life and in the life to come, is based on this gospel testimony.

Q. 85 How is the kingdom of heaven closed and opened by Christian discipline?
A. According to the command of Christ: Those who, though called Christians, profess unchristian teachings or live unchristian lives, and who after repeated personal and loving admonitions, refuse to abandon their errors and evil ways, and who after being reported to the church, that is, to those ordained by the church for that purpose, fail to respond also to the church's admonitions – such persons the church excludes from the Christian community by withholding the sacraments from them, and God also excludes them from the kingdom of Christ. Such persons, when promising and demonstrating genuine reform, are received again as members of Christ and of his church.

As we have noticed several times, the Heidelberg Catechism understands God's grace as gift *and* claim upon the believer, and interprets the believers' only comfort of belonging to God not only as assurance, but also as task. Accordingly, the Heidelberg Catechism concludes its section on the sacraments and with this also the second part on deliverance with a discussion of the "keys of the kingdom" as a prolongation of the doctrine of sacraments and the Eucharistic life. This concept of the keys of kingdom (also known as keys of *heaven*) is taken from Mt 16:19 and John 20:22–23, and refers not to papal authority as in the Roman Catholic church, but to the office of the church and all of its members in dealing with the very real and pressing problem of those people who confess to be Christians, yet demonstrate by their lives to be "hypocrites, unbelieving and unrepentant". The catechism identifies two keys to open the kingdom of heaven for believers and to close it for unbelievers: the first one being, rather unspectacularly so, the regular praxis of preaching, and the second one being Christian (or church) discipline towards repentance. Before we have a look at those two keys one after other, we need to take a moment in order to avoid a rather common misunderstanding. Even though the keys of heaven are confessed to open and close the kingdom of Christ, and even though those keys are in the hands of the church, they neither cause forgiveness of sins by admitting believers to the sacraments, nor exclude unbelievers from the forgiveness of sins by excluding them from the sacraments. Forgiveness of sins was gained through Jesus Christ's death on the cross, once and for all; it does not depend on baptism, the Lord's Supper or any other church praxis, as the Heidelberg Catechism kept emphasizing constantly especially in its section on the sacraments. The church does not assume what is and remains beyond doubt only *God's,* because it is God, who because of *Christ's merit* truly forgives all sins, as question 84 states. Yet by the command of Christ, the church as the communion of pardoned sinners has to assume a responsibility for all of her members. Accepting this mutual responsibility does not mean to assume a "holier-than-thou" posture, quite the contrary, but it also means to reject all forms of indifferent "anything-goes" attitudes. It is primarily an inner-church responsibility, it is first and foremost about "us" and not about "them"; it is about those who are members of the church and confess themselves to be Christians. The office of the keys is, in fact, a matter of *pastoral care* for the whole congregation, for those who recognize their need for forgiveness as well as for those who do not.

In the preaching of the holy gospel this two-fold perspective is easily discernable: to those who accept the gospel promise of forgiveness of sins with true faith, it is proclaimed and publicly declared that they are *truly* forgiven. Each and every believer may trust in God's promise of grace, may experience the comfort of belonging to God, and would not need to fear God's judgment on her or his sins; this is the core message of each sermon according to the Heidelberg Catechism, because it is the core message of the holy gospel. In that sense, and only that sense, the church opens the kingdom of Christ to all believers in pronouncing it open for them. Unrepentant hypocrites and unbelievers, those who do not have true faith, who do not trust completely in God, but dismiss God's grace, have already excluded themselves from the church of the pardoned sinners. They are called to repent, to turn around towards God, and if they continue with their rejection of God's grace, the church is called to proclaim and publicly declare that their behavior has indeed dire consequences for them.

Christian discipline, the second key, is also directed first of all at repentance, not at exclusion. Yet if the church sees no repentance and reform, exclusion might be the called for reaction of the church – after going through a process of carefully devised steps of "repeated personal and loving admonitions" by those who are chosen by the church for that reason. Those who "profess unchristian teachings or live unchristian lives", although they call themselves Christians, are to be excluded from the sacraments; not because they are sinners, since *all* members of the church are sinners and are, because of that, called to the Lord's Supper. They are to be excluded because they *live* their lives contrary to God's gift of grace, or because they *teach* a comfortless doctrine contrary to God's gift of grace. Note, how both orthodoxy (right teaching) as well as orthopraxis (right living) are the goal of Christian discipline, and errors in both are offensive to God in the same way. (The third part of the catechism, especially in its exposition of the Ten Commandments, will give us a deeper and detailed insight of what the Heidelberg Catechism considers as "right living"). As said above, Christian discipline should not be confused with moralism or any other feeling of superiority; it is to be understood and practiced as loving counsel, as a life-giving and not life-denying discipline in solidarity with other sinners. For that reason, the last sentence of question 86, which is also the last sentence of the second part on deliverance, ends with the promise of graceful forgiveness and return to the church for those who leave their grace-less ways and accept God's gift of grace.

Part III: Gratitude

The third part of the Heidelberg Catechism develops the strange logic of grace further: those who belong to God in life and death, who know the misery of their sin and the joy of their deliverance, and who accept God's grace in true faith as gift and claim, confess that the Holy Spirit makes them "wholeheartedly willing and ready from now on to live for him" (question 1). What does it look like to live for God in the joy of God's comfort (question 2)? Forty-four questions (more than a third of the whole catechism) and 21 Lord's Days have been devoted to the very practical consequences and fruits of the true faith. And although the Heidelberg Catechism does not really add new theological material in this part, but rather works on the foundation of what has been said before, this translation of doctrinal statements into the context of every-day life in the 16th century is particularly instructive and inspiring also for us, even though our context could not be more different from theirs. Over this gap of 450 years, we recognize that we, too, are called to find our ways of living in right relationship with God and neighbor, just like the believers in the Palatinate then and there. The fact, therefore, that this introduction does not discuss the third part of the Heidelberg Catechism as extensively as the first two parts does not indicate a lesser appreciation of it, but is simply the result of subsuming thematically similar issues under the same subsection in order to clarify and emphasize the main insights and challenges we find here on the basis of what has been developed before.

Lord's Day 32 (86–87): Restoration and Thankful Lives

Q. 86 Since we have been delivered from our misery by grace through Christ without any merit of our own, why then should we do good works?

A. Because Christ, having redeemed us by his blood, is also restoring us by his Spirit into his image, so that with our whole lives we may show that we are thankful to God for his benefits, so that he may be praised through us, so that we may be assured of our faith by its fruits, and so that by our godly living our neighbors may be won over to Christ.

> Q. 87 Can those be saved who do not turn to God from their ungrate-
> ful and unrepentant ways?
> A. By no means. Scripture tells us that no unchaste person, no idol-
> ater, adulterer, thief, no covetous person, no drunkard, slanderer,
> robber, or the like will inherit the kingdom of God.

Summing up what has been said before in parts I (misery) and II
(deliverance), the third part on gratitude begins with a statement that
once again applies the Reformation watchwords of *sola gratia* and
solus Christus; we are saved through Christ alone by grace alone. What
consequences does this being saved have for our way of live; what are
good works good for? In this question, we hear not only the challenge
of Roman Catholic opponents, but also the voice of troubled and
confused believers of the Reformation century. Already Question 64
asked in a similar way whether this teaching of righteousness does
not make people indifferent and wicked, and answered with reference
to our being engrafted in Christ and the fruits of gratitude, in short:
to the work of the Holy Spirit. Question 86 now takes up this line of
thought and specifies it. We have heard, especially in the section dealing with the sacraments, how blood and Spirit of Christ have worked
and are working in, on and for us, and this concept is applied here
again relating it to *our* past, presence, and future. Jesus Christ, by his
blood, has already redeemed us, once and for all, in the past event of
the cross. This is the one and only basis for our understanding of what
good works are and why we should do them: the motivation for them
can not and need not lie in any attempt to gain merit from them. This
is the first part of the comfort of belonging to God, as question 1 has
stated it. We do good because we *may,* not because we *must* (Allen
Verhey). The second part of this comfort lies in the work of Christ's
Spirit, who is restoring us to Christ's image, who is working on us
right here and now, and will remain with us forever (question 53),
renewing us more and more after God's image (question 115). We
are restored, reconstituted, recreated, so that because of this second
creation we can begin living the life God has created us for: in true
righteousness and holiness, knowing, loving, praising, and glorifying God (question 6), and the fruits of gratitude this Eucharistic life
produces are the good works done out of true faith.

Yet the initial question is still not answered: what are good works good for? The Heidelberg Catechism gives us a fourfold answer to this question; we do good works in order a) to demonstrate our gratitude for God's gifts of grace, b) to praise God, c) to be assured of our faith, and, finally, d) to win our neighbor over to Christ.

a) In *all sections* of our lives we are enabled to lead the new Eucharistic life and to demonstrate our gratitude: in family, marriage, and social relations of all kinds, in politics, economics, work place, church, and so on. The discussion of the Decalogue, the Lord's Prayer, and their implications for each and every believer's daily life will explicate how the authors of the Heidelberg Catechism understood this grateful belonging to God in terms of the context of real life in the 16th century, sometimes obviously in a very time-bound way, but always trying to live according to the promise of renewal by the Holy Spirit. b) One of the ultimate goals of human living is, as we have seen already in question 6, to praise and glorify God, and in this, the Heidelberg Catechism reflects a common and central Reformed emphasis. In the context of good works this emphasis on *Soli Deo Gloria* (to God alone be glory) means: our works are good only if through them we praise and honor the gracious God, and not seek our own praise, honor, or any other merit – not from God and not from other humans. c) The good works as fruits of faith now may also serve in assuring us of our faith. How so? In true faith, we understand that we need not justify ourselves by our own good works, that we may rely on God's grace completely, that our response to this grace is gratitude. Grateful good works, then, point us back not to ourselves and all sorts of self-doubts and fruitless attempts of justifying ourselves, but to God's reliable gift of grace and the comfort we receive through the work of the Holy Spirit. d) The last aspect adds a new perspective not only to this section on good works, but to the whole catechism; a perspective which we may call "missional", to use a contemporary expression. We do good works in order not to impress our neighbors and make them praise us and our godly lives, but it order to "win them over" to Christ. In reflecting God's grace, our good works may point others to the source of all good, witnessing to the gift of grace we have received and now aim to share with others. Good works thus become an instrument of mission.

Question 87 reiterates what has already been said in the previous section on the kingdom of keys: for those who, despite all admonitions and loving counsel, do not repent and leave their unbelieving ways the kingdom of heaven is closed. Not because they are sinners, since all are sinners, or because they would be worse sinners than others, since God does not know of "better sinners" and "worse sinners", but because they are *impenitent* and *unthankful* sinners, not trusting in God's grace and not willing to lead the Eucharistic life of continual repentance. Consequently, the Heidelberg Catechism moves on to a discussion of how to understand *and* live conversion.

Lord's Day 33 (88–91): Conversion and Good Works

> Q. 88 What is involved in genuine repentance or conversion?
> A. Two things: the dying-away of the old self, and the rising-to-life of the new.
>
> Q. 89 What is the dying-away of the old self?
> A. To be genuinely sorry for sin and more and more to hate and run away from it.
>
> Q. 90 What is the rising-to-life of the new self?
> A. Wholehearted joy in God through Christ and a love and delight to live according to the will of God by doing every kind of good work.
>
> Q. 91 What are good works?
> A. Only those which are done out of true faith, conform to God's law, and are done for God's glory; and not those based on our own opinion or human tradition.

Our turning away from our ungrateful and unrepentant ways is our conversion as our grateful response to God's gift of grace, and it consists in two different acts: the dying-away of the old self and the rising-to-life of the new. And even though conversion is indeed *our* response, it is based upon a Christological foundation: we benefit from Christ's death and resurrection in that by Christ's power "our old selves are crucified, put to death, and buried with him" (question 43) and in that "we too are already raised to a new life" (question 45). By Christ's power in this one-time event on the cross, we have already been made right with God, and we need not repeat what Christ has already done for us. Neither is conversion a kind of pre-condition for receiving God's grace; it is already a result of receiving God's grace! We are justified, but God continues to work in, on, with, and for us in making us holy, sanctifying us, renewing and restoring us. Accordingly, in our conversion, our turning to God and God alone, we do not cause our justification or make it effective, we do in no way redeem ourselves, but we affirm our deliverance out of the misery of sin through Christ's merit. And since we never leave sin behind us completely, but will always remain sinners (yet pardoned sinners), conversion, too, is no one-time event or decision, but in fact describes an entire life of continual repentance, as already Martin Luther emphasized in the first of his famous 95 theses. Christian life is a perfect *Christian* life, if it is a life of daily new beginnings despite all remaining imperfections, and not a life in static and unwavering impeccability.

Consequently, being genuinely sorry for sin, hating it and running away from it, as question 89 puts it, is a perpetual task for every believer. We may indeed, hopefully, see improvement in our lives, indicated by the "more and more" the Heidelberg Catechism uses here, but we will never be entirely without sin, remaining always in need of God's grace and always with the promise of God's grace. The gospel command of "repent and turn to God!" can only be understood together with the declaration "Your sins are forgiven!" Dying-away of the old self, thus, is a continuing process based upon the one-time event of Christ's cross, and therefore a grace-filled process – as is the rising-to-life of the new self also based upon the one-time event of Christ's resurrection. What does this new life look like, this continual, thankful turning to God and turning away from our impenitent ways? Question 90 provides us with a beautiful description, which differs quite a bit from many gloomy, sententious or moralistic portrayals of the life of repentant believers: it is wholehearted joy, love, and delight! A joy in God through Christ, love and delight that flow from living according to the will of God – those are the markers of Christian life, and not frustration, depression, pride, or fear. We can live and die in the comfort of belonging to God (question 2), by thanking God for our deliverance from the misery of sin and by living a life of gratitude, doing good works that are *good* for us and others. So the Heidelberg Catechism asks, recapitulating what has been said before about good works, "What are good works?", and provides us with a concise and memorable answer: good works are those that are done out of true faith – acknowledging that they are grateful responses to God's grace and in no way earn this grace; and which ultimately do what we have been created for: praise God. And a third element is mentioned in this answer, which the Heidelberg Catechism will deal with in detail (in more than twenty questions and on 11 Lord's Days) in the following section on the Ten Commandments: good works are those which follow God's rules and commands, not human opinions and traditions. With the help of God's law, we are instructed on how to live our daily lives in a Eucharistic way; God's law teaches us God's loving and graceful will for our lives. This inherently positive understanding of the law of God is distinctively Reformed, and has been called the "third use of the law", the use of the law for the believers, who are already renewed by the work of the Holy Spirit. We have encountered the "first use of the law" (convicting us of our sin and teaching us our need of grace) in part II on human misery; the second use of the law (sometimes transposed with the first use) is its political or civil function. We have already noted above that the Heidelberg Catechism espouses an ethic of gratitude, and we see in this understanding of the law as the expression of God's love for us the foundation for this kind of ethics based not on fear of punishment, but on the free, responsible, thankful response of the justified and sanctified believer.

The Ten Commandments

Lord's Day 34 (92-93): The Law of God

Q. 92 What is God's law?
A. God spoke all these words:
THE FIRST COMMANDMENT: "I am the LORD your God, who brought

you out of the land of Egypt, out of the house of slavery; you shall have no other gods before me."

THE SECOND COMMANDMENT: "You shall not make for yourself an idol, whether in form of anything that is in heaven above, or that is on the earth beneath, or that is in the water under the earth. You shall not bow down to them or worship them; for I the LORD your God am a jealous God, punishing children for the iniquity of parents, to the third and fourth generation of those who reject me, but showing love to the thousandth generation of those who love me and keep my commandments."

THE THIRD COMMANDMENT: "You shall not make wrongful use of the name of the LORD your God, for the LORD will not acquit anyone who misuses his name."

THE FOURTH COMMANDMENT: "Remember the Sabbath day and keep it holy. Six days you shall labor and do all your work. But the seventh day is a Sabbath to the LORD your God; you shall not do any work – you, your son or your daughter, your male or female slave, your livestock, or the alien resident in your towns. For in six days the LORD made the heaven and earth, the sea, and all that is in them, but rested the seventh day; therefore the LORD blessed the Sabbath day and consecrated it."

THE FIFTH COMMANDMENT: "Honor your father and your mother, so that your days may be long in the land that the LORD your God is giving to you."

THE SIXTH COMMANDMENT: "You shall not murder."

THE SEVENTH COMMANDMENT: "You shall not commit adultery."

THE EIGHTH COMMANDMENT: "You shall not steal."

THE NINTH COMMANDMENT: "You shall not bear false witness against your neighbor."

THE TENTH COMMANDMENT: "You shall not covet your neighbor's house; you shall not covet your neighbor's wife, or male or female slave, or ox, or donkey, or anything that belongs to your neighbor."

Q. 93 How are these commandments divided?
A. Into two tables. The first has four commandments, teaching us how we ought to live in relation to God. The second has six commandments, teaching us what we owe our neighbor.

God's self-introduction as Liberator right at the beginning sets the tone for all that follows: The context of the law is *deliverance;* the law-giver is the *deliverer* – this is what the First commandment emphatically emphasizes, and with this it sets the tone for all commandments that follow. And this is what the Heidelberg Catechism emphasizes together with the Decalogue; this is the reason why it discusses the Decalogue under the theme of gratitude: we have been delivered from our misery of sin "out of sheer grace", and the law, in the form of the ten commandments, is the "shape of God's permission to life a new life" (Allen Verhey). Thus the law can never be truly understood without its inherent relation to God's grace, a grace that comes as gift and claim. We belong to God in all areas of our lives, all the time, and there is no sphere where we would not be under God's promise and claim. In all realms of our lives, we are to *and* may trust God alone as those who are freed by God and who participate in the covenant of freedom established by God. Questions 94 to 115 will discuss this active and obedient freedom in community, for and in relationship with God and others (Eberhard Busch) in detail, spelling out concretely for the context of the 16th century, and maybe also for ours, what it means to belong to God.

In question 4, the Heidelberg Catechism has already given us an interpretative key in order to understand the law of God and what we are required to do: the Twofold Law of God teaches us to love God with all our heart, soul, and mind, and to love our neighbor as ourselves. The fulfillment of the law is not to be found in a perfunctory observance of rules and regulations, not even in strictly sticking to the letters of the Decalogue. The fulfillment of the law is love [Rom 13:10] – love of God and love of neighbor. The law of God as God's gift of love guides us to live in right and loving community with God and human beings; and the two tables of the law deal with living our loving relation with God (1–4) and with our neighbor (5–10), respectively. Conversely, with this understanding of the law, we recognize our sin not only as offense against God, but also as offense against our neighbor. In that sense, we do not assess our "keeping the law" in terms of how many of the Ten Commandments we are breaking, or how good we are in keeping them, but to which extent all of our life reflects God's love and grace in completely relying on God's love and grace. No one, not even the holiest, will ever be able to keep the commandments perfectly, but we "never stop striving and praying to God for the grace of the Holy Spirit, to be renewed more and more after God's image", as question 115 says as a conclusion of the discussion of the Ten Commandments.

One brief remark on the numbering of commandments: at the time of the Reformation, not only the understanding of the law and its uses (Luther, for example, did not explicitly teach a third use of the law), but also the numbering of the commandments was a controversial matter. Whereas Lutheran and Roman Catholic churches combine the prohibition of other gods and the prohibition of idolatry into one commandment, or even omit the prohibition of idolatry, Reformed, Anglican, and Orthodox Churches count those two prohibitions as two commandments. In order to keep the number of *Ten* Commandments, Lutheran and Roman Catholic churches split the prohibition of coveting into two, while Reformed churches consider it one commandment. The Heidelberg Catechism, obviously, follows the Reformed numbering of commandments.

Lord's Day 34 cont. –38 (94–103): The First Table – Living the Loving Relation with God

Q. 94 What does the Lord require in the first commandment?
A. That I, not wanting to endanger my own salvation, avoid and shun all idolatry, sorcery, superstitious rites, and prayer to saints or to other creatures. That I rightly know the only true God, trust him alone, and look to God for every good thing humbly and patiently, and love, fear, and honor God with all my heart. In short, that I give up anything rather than go against God's will in any way.

Q. 95 What is idolatry?
A. Idolatry is having or inventing something in which one trusts in place of or alongside of the only true God, who has revealed himself in the Word.

Q. 96 What is God's will for us in the second commandment?
A. That we in no way make any image of God nor worship him in any other way than has been commanded in God's Word.

Q. 97 May we then not make any image at all?

A. God can not and may not be visibly portrayed in any way. Although creatures may be portrayed, yet God forbids making or having such images if one's intention is to worship them or to serve God through them.

Q. 98 But may not images be permitted in churches in place of books for the unlearned?

A. No, we should not try to be wiser than God. God wants the Christian community instructed by the living preaching of his Word – not by idols that cannot even talk.

Q. 99 What is the aim of the third commandment?

A. That we neither blaspheme nor misuse the name of God by cursing, perjury, or unnecessary oaths, nor share in such horrible sins by being silent bystanders. In summary, we should use the holy name of God only with reverence and awe, so that we may properly confess God, pray to God, and glorify God in all our words and works.

Q. 100 Is blasphemy of God's name by swearing and cursing really such serious sin that God is angry also with those who do not do all they can to help prevent and forbid it?

A. Yes, indeed. No sin is greater or provokes God's wrath more than blaspheming his name. That is why God commanded it to be punished with death.

Q. 101 But may we swear an oath in God's name if we do it reverently?

A. Yes, when the government demands it, or when necessity requires it, in order to maintain and promote truth and trustworthiness for God's glory and our neighbor's good. Such oaths are grounded in God's Word and were rightly used by the people of God in the Old and New Testaments.

Q. 102 May we also swear by saints or other creatures?

A. No. A legitimate oath means calling upon God as the only one who knows my heart to witness to my truthfulness and to punish me if I swear falsely. No creature is worthy of such honor.

> Q. 103 What is God's will for you in the fourth commandment?
> A. First, that the gospel ministry and education for it be maintained, and that, especially on the festive day of rest, I diligently attend the assembly of God's people to learn what God's Word teaches, to participate in the sacraments, to pray to God publicly, and to bring Christian offerings for the poor. Second, that every day of my life I rest from my evil ways, let the Lord work in me through his Spirit, and so begin in this life the eternal Sabbath.

Dealing now with the first table of the Decalogue and our loving relation with God, we will notice how these questions are indeed concerned with God, yet do not neglect our relation to our neighbors as well. The two tables cannot be separated from each other, since there are not two isolated "loves" fulfilling the law, but there is only one love in two relations. How, then, do we live this loving relation to God? The first commandment, or "permission", is concerned with the ultimate goal of our trusting love: God, the Deliverer, the only true God, the One who has revealed Godself to us in the Word, is the One we are permitted to love, fear, and honor. This God, who is our almighty and loving Father, our brother in Christ, and our comforter in the Holy Spirit, who graciously gathers, protects and preserves us, bids us to respond by trusting in God alone – not in any concept or notion (of God or whatsoever) we or others have invented, and which become idols for us by claiming our ultimate trust. Trusting not in the only true God but in other gods takes on different forms in different ages, and our idolatries may very well differ quite a lot from the list given in question 94; yet all idolatries share one essential precondition: with these idolatries we do not only replace God as God has revealed Godself to us with an idol, but in doing so, we surrender ourselves to "the house of slavery" we have been delivered from: the comfort-less and grace-less home of self-deifying, self-justification, and self-reliance, because these self-made idols cannot but ultimately refer us back to ourselves. There is no true living and loving "You" in the relation to an idol, only an "I" in various forms and shapes. The prohibition of having no other gods before the Lord, then, is the permission to live in true relationship with the only true God.

That idolatry was indeed a central issue of the Reformed reformation becomes obvious by looking at the discussion of the second
commandment in questions 96–98, which also deal with the same
issue from a different perspective. Whereas the first commandment
in the interpretation of the Heidelberg Catechism prohibits *replacing
God* with idols, the second commandment prohibits *making God
into* an idol according to our respective perceptions and prejudices.
Idol-making results in worshipping and serving those idols, and those
human-made images of God exercise power of us, demanding our
loyalty and love, thus leading us away from encountering and obeying
the true God. We do not relate in love to the living reality of God,
but to an abstract, human-made concept of God, be it in the form of
an image of a saint, a church wall painting (existential problems for
Protestant churches in the 16th century), or a theological teaching that
is not based on God's revelation but on human ideas. According to
the Heidelberg Catechism, however, the second commandment also
contains a positive statement: we are not left to our own resources
and devices, since we are given the necessary aid to truly worship
and serve God in the *living preaching* of God's Word. Reading question 95 and 98 together, and keeping question 65 in mind (the Spirit
produces faith in us through the preaching of the holy gospel), we
realize that we need not, cannot, and should not try to capture and
domesticate God, but that God comes to us: God revealed Godself
to us in the Word and instructs us through the preaching of this
Word. As Calvin commented in his *Institutes,* "God himself is the
sole and proper witness of himself!" Thus we love, honor, and fear
God by not trying to be wiser than God, but by letting *God* speak
for and about *God.*

Only to the third commandment the Heidelberg Catechism
devotes two Lord's Days – an indication of how serious the catechism takes this issue. What is at stake here? In the background of
this discussion we find the very same concern we have encountered
in the previous commandments, which is, stated positively, that we
might rightly serve God, and, stated negatively, that we may not
use God in our service for our own goals by misusing and manip-
ulating God's name. God's name is God's trustworthy and steadfast
presence with us as the Deliverer, God introduces Godself to us in

sovereignty and holiness in order to establish community with us. Misusing God's name in any form, thus, presupposes that not only God's name is at our disposal, but Godself, and this constitutes not only a denial of but also an assault on God's sovereignty and holiness. According to the Heidelberg Catechism, this is such a serious sin against God, it so harms not only our loving relation to God, but also to our neighbors, that we are not only called to refrain from it ourselves, but also called to take on responsibility for this misuse by others – we are not allowed to retreat into a spectator position as "silent bystanders". Instead, we are called to "use the holy name of God only with reference and awe", because all of our life, all the time, in words and works, has but one goal: to glorify God. In its exposition of the first petition of the Lord's prayer, question 122 will explain more fully what the right use of God's name looks like, but already right here we see how central this question is for the Heidelberg Catechism's understanding of the right relationship to God. Martin Luther's Large Catechism in its comment on this commandment, which, according to Luther, "leads us outward and directs the mouth and tongue to God", remarks quite illuminatingly why words in general, and God's name in particular, are not merely sounds and noise in commenting that "the first objects that spring from the heart and manifest themselves are words." Our words, then, stand in direct relationship with our hearts as the seat of our love of God. So we may use God's name reverently and even swear an oath in God's name (which was prohibited in the more radical wings of the Reformation out of fear of misusing God's name), as long as we are truly pursuing the goal of promoting truth and trustworthiness, with the twofold aim of glorifying God *and* furthering our neighbor's good. (As a side note, in this permission of the government to demand an oath of its citizens, we see an example of the second use of the law in its civil or political use.)

Even though we might think at first that the fourth commandment is primarily about the believers' Sunday rest and not about God, the Heidelberg Catechism counts it in the first table and our relationship to God. As those who are set free by God and brought into the community of God's people, we are invited to respond to God's gracious actions in *worship* and *life*. The catechism begins by underlining the importance of gospel ministry (the ministry of preaching) and education (instruction in the Christian faith) in general, and continues by listing the four constitutive elements of Christian worship service: sermon, sacraments, public prayer, and offering for the needy. As members of God's community, we not only relate to God in love, but to all of God's people as well. Thus the fourth commandment has explicit social implications for all churches, every day of the week, as the second part of the answer states: God's eternal Sabbath begins already here and now in our staying away from evil ways *every day*, letting the Spirit work in us. Sabbath observance, consequently, is not about prohibitions and "do's and don'ts" to begin with, but about the gift of the festive day of rest, of celebrating God's grace in community and for the community. In summary, the Sabbath is about the new life, which is already fulfilled in Christ's resurrection, and of which we are already part of the rising-to-life of our new selves. Therefore, most Christian churches celebrate the Sabbath on the first day of the week, the Lord's Day and day of Christ's resurrection, looking back to the first Easter Sunday and forward to the eternal Sabbath.

Lord's Day 39–44 (104–115): The Second Table – Living the Loving Relation with Our Neighbor

Q. 104 What is God's will for you in the fifth commandment?
A. That I honor, love, and be loyal to my father and mother and all those in authority over me; that I submit myself with proper obedience to all their good teaching and discipline; and also that I be patient with their failings – for through them God chooses to rule us.

Q. 105 What is God's will for you in the sixth commandment?
A. I am not to belittle, hate, insult, or kill my neighbor – not by my thoughts, my words, my look or gesture, and certainly not by actual deeds – and I am not to be party to this in others; rather, I am to put away all desire for revenge. I am not to harm or recklessly endanger myself either. Prevention of murder is also why government is armed with the sword.

Q. 106 Does this commandment refer only to murder?

A. By forbidding murder God teaches us that he hates the root of murder: envy, hatred, anger, vindictiveness. In God's sight all such are murder.

Q. 107 Is it enough then that we do not murder our neighbor in any such way?

A. No. By condemning envy, hatred, and anger God wants us to love our neighbors as ourselves, to be patient, peace-loving, gentle, merciful, and friendly toward them, to protect them from harm as much as we can, and to do good even to our enemies.

Q. 108 What does the seventh commandment teach us?

A. That God condemns all unchastity, and that therefore we should thoroughly detest it and live decent and chaste lives, within or outside of the holy state of marriage.

Q. 109 Does God, in this commandment, forbid only such scandalous sins as adultery?

A. We are temples of the Holy Spirit, body and soul, and God wants both to be kept clean and holy. That is why God forbids all unchaste actions, looks, talk, thoughts, or desires, and whatever may incite someone to them.

Q. 110 What does God forbid in the eighth commandment?

A. God forbids not only outright theft and robbery, punishable by law. But in God's sight theft also includes all scheming and swindling in order to get our neighbor's goods for ourselves, whether by force or means that appear legitimate, such as inaccurate measurements of weight, size, or volume; fraudulent merchandising; counterfeit money; excessive interest; or any other means forbidden by God. In addition God forbids all greed and pointless squandering of his gifts.

Q. 111 What does God require of you in this commandment?

A. That I do whatever I can for my neighbor's good, that I treat others as I would like them to treat me, and that I work faithfully so that I may share with those in need.

Q. 112 What is the aim of the ninth commandment?
A. That I never give false testimony against anyone, twist no one's words, not gossip or slander, nor join in condemning anyone rashly or without a hearing. Rather, in court and everywhere else, I should avoid lying and deceit of every kind; these are the very devices the devil uses, and they would call down on me God's intense wrath. I should love the truth, speak it candidly, and openly acknowledge it. And I should do what I can to guard and advance my neighbor's good name.

Q. 113 What is the aim of the tenth commandment?
A. That not even the slightest desire or thought contrary to any one of God's commandments should ever arise in our hearts. Rather, with all our hearts we should always hate sin and take pleasure in whatever is right.

Q. 114 But can those converted to God obey these commandments perfectly?
A. No. In this life even the holiest have only a small beginning of this obedience. Nevertheless, with all seriousness of purpose, they do begin to live according to all, not only some, of God's commandments.

Q. 115 Since no one in this life can obey the Ten Commandments perfectly, why does God want them preached so pointedly?
A. First, so that the longer we live the more we may come to know our sinfulness and the more eagerly look to Christ for forgiveness of sins and righteousness. Second, so that, we may never stop striving, and never stop praying to God for the grace of the Holy Spirit, to be renewed more and more after God's image, until after this life we reach our goal: perfection.

With the second table and its emphasis on our loving relation to our neighbors, the Heidelberg Catechism illustrates in detail what our life of gratitude can and should look like. We have already noticed in several places how the Heidelberg Catechism includes all spheres of our life into the true service of God, not restricting it to the so-called religious sphere: we belong to God with body and soul, all the time and everywhere, and this costly comfort has direct consequences for our life. Accordingly, our love of neighbor is not a mere private and subjective sentiment or attitude, but "active involvement in the existence of others for the furtherance of their well-being" (Eberhard Busch), which implies mercy *and* justice in reflecting God's grace as mercy and justice. It is important to keep in mind what we have said above: the context of the law is *grace;* the grace of God which enables us to live truly and faithful human lives. So what is true for both tables becomes particularly important for the second table: the catechism is not meant to be used as a kind of yardstick of our performance, in order to either judge or congratulate ourselves, depending on our failures or achievements. We are not Christians because we lead an impeccable Christian life, and we remain Christians even though we do not lead an impeccable Christian life (impeccable understood here in the original sense of "incapable of sin"); we are and remain Christians, because we share in Christ's anointing in order "to present ourselves to him as a living sacrifice of thanks and to strive with a free conscience against sin and the devil in this life" (question 32). Questions 104–115 aim to provide us with a guide to this kind of Eucharistic living.

The fifth commandment discusses our relationship with our parents and "all those in authority over me", understanding our relationship with them in terms of love, honor, and loyalty. The Heidelberg Catechism claims that all authorities serve a particular purpose, and this purpose is the essential reason for and limit of their authority over us: God has chosen to rule us through them, and since we know what kind of ruler God is as our God and Father because of Christ the Son (questions 26–28), we know that God's rule is indeed a good rule. Our reaction to legitimate authorities, then, is submitting ourselves with *proper* obedience to all their *good* teaching and discipline. The two adjectives "proper" and "good" indicate a crucial reservation, though: despite the postulated patience with the failings of authorities, there is a limit to our loyalty, since we owe absolute loyalty only to God – as the Heidelberg Catechism emphasized over and over again in its discussion of the first table. It is our task, then, and no easy one at that, to judge the claim of all authorities on our lives and to work out whether they are legitimate claims reflecting God's rule or whether the authorities have turned into idols, keeping in mind that we always must obey God rather than any human authority [Acts 5:29].

The sixth commandment, a short commandment with its mere four words, requires a rather lengthy exposition in three questions, because, for the Heidelberg Catechism, God's will in this commandment is not restricted to the prohibition of the outward act of physically killing another person. The catechism challenges us to consider the underlying root of murder (envy, hatred, anger, vindictiveness), and explicates what our loving relation to our neighbor is called to look like in detail. In doing so, the Heidelberg Catechism gives us a fine example of how interpreting the Ten Commandments with the interpretative key of the twofold love does not stick to the letter of the commandment, but rather tries to find out how we could best serve God in serving our neighbors. Therefore the catechism, in its quite realistic attitude towards people and their "natural tendency to hate God and my neighbor" (question 5), extends the meaning of "killing" to all forms of demeaning, discriminating, and antagonistic behavior, whether they are carried out in deeds, words, look, gesture or thought, in accordance with Christ's own proclamation in the Sermon on the Mount. A rather sobering list for most of us, who might take pride in never actually hurting other people, much less murdering them. And again, the Heidelberg Catechism does not allow for a spectator position where we would tolerate or ignore assaults on others, since we are called "to protect our neighbors from harm as much as we can". Question 105 demands nothing less than the absolute respect for human life, including my own life, in all its facets. Prevention of murder and protection of human life, therefore, is the reason why the government is armed with the sword; quite similar to what we have seen earlier, the authorities are assigned a particular purpose in order to carry out God's will. Because envy, hatred, anger, and vindictiveness are the breeding ground for murder, God condemns them, according to question 107, and commands, invites, and permits us to truly love our neighbors as ourselves. It is not enough to not kill, we are called to proactively create a basic situation characterized by patience, love of peace, gentleness, mercy, and friendliness – in short, we are called to reflect God's grace in our attitude and behavior towards our neighbors, who are human beings created in God's image, just like us.

The Heidelberg Catechism's exposition of the seventh commandment continues with this line of interpretation following the Sermon on the Mount in condemning not only the physical act of adultery, but all that leads to it and prepares the ground for unfaithfulness or indecencies. Why is that? We belong to God, body *and* soul, and because both are the temple of the Holy Spirit, God demands that we keep them clean and holy. Being sanctified by the Holy Spirit and called to live holy lives, Christians may enjoy God's good gifts in a responsible and loving way, respecting body and soul of the other as well as their own. It is obvious that holiness and cleanliness are depicted here from an 16th century understanding of "unchastity", and that each time and age has to find its own faithful interpretation of what it means to be the temple of the Holy Spirit, body and soul. It is also obvious, though, that Heidelberg Catechism does not argue for or against a particular morality or set of moral values, but it wants to redirect our gaze at God's command that is to be fulfilled in love as are all other commandments.

In a similar and even more detailed way, the interpretation of the eighth commandment does not only prohibit outright stealing, but calls for and invites to our love of neighbor in all economic and social relationships. Standing up for economic and social justice, doing whatever we can do for our neighbors' good, therefore, is not an option among others, but flows right out of our love to God and gratitude for God's gifts of grace. Just like before, the command *not to do* one thing contains, according to the Heidelberg Catechism, the demand of doing another: serving our neighbors in love. The law of God is filled positively, because the rising-to-life of the new self enables us to live the new life in God's grace, for God's glory and for the good of our neighbor. And this is true for all economic dimensions of our life, too, for which the Heidelberg Catechism provides us with an interesting glance at typical fraudulent transactions of the 16th century such as inaccurate measurements or excessive interest. Unfortunately, this 450-year old list contains some still current practices, and could easily be extended by contemporary, sophisticated or primitive, economic fraudulences. A life of gratitude, then, is a life of truthfulness and solidarity, even to the point that our work is understood, first of all, as a means to be able to support those in need. Living from the comfort of belonging to God would certainly change also the way we perceive all financial, economic, and social transactions and relations, with Allen Verhey asking, capturing the intention of the Heidelberg Catechism quite accurately, "what an economic system would look like if we had the courage of comfort?".

By now, we are already familiar with the Heidelberg Catechism's approach in stating negatively what a commandment prohibits, and then stating positively how we fulfill this commandment in love. The exposition of the ninth commandment follows the same procedure in first listing all we have to avoid, not only in court, but in all of our life: all forms of lying and deceit, from false testimony to simple gossip. Those are the instruments of the devil, the father of lies [John 8:44]; our Father in heaven, however, is reliable, loving and graceful *truth*, which we are called, permitted, and enabled to reflect in word, deed, and mind. We are capable of loving and living the truth, because we have been engrafted into Christ, who is the Truth, and who has given us the Spirit of Truth. Loving our neighbor in loving the truth, then, does not only mean to passively refrain from telling lies, but to actively engage in protecting and furthering my neighbor's good name, publicly recognizing and speaking the truth in love [Eph 4:15]. This love of truth has direct and complex implications for our way of life, reaching from due process for everyone by not "condemning anyone rashly or without a hearing" to truth-in-advertising campaigns by avoiding "lying and deceit of every kind". Love, as the fulfillment of the law, will take on many forms and shapes in our daily life, and it is our task to continuously mold these forms and shapes according to God's good will.

Question 113 concludes the interpretation of the Decalogue with a rather unexpected exposition of the tenth commandment. Instead of explaining the prohibition of coveting with reference to the mentioned "objects" of desire, the Heidelberg Catechism understands it (like Calvin) as a kind of *summary of the whole law* and its gracious intention for us. Understanding covetousness as the cause and root of all our sins (Fred Klooster), the interpretation of the tenth commandment helps us to discern the basic meaning of all commandments on both tables: we are to be so filled with love of God and neighbor, that we neither think of nor desire anything "contrary to any one of God's commandments" – we are totally God's, belonging to God, body and soul. God's gracious law enables us not only to always (recognize and) hate our sin, but also to take pleasure in doing what is right. What an astounding claim this is: following God's law, God's commandments, is not a burden, but a delight and joy! With the words of question 90, it is the *rising-to-life of the new self* that brings us not only "wholehearted joy in God through Christ", but also "a love and delight to live according to the will of God by doing every kind of good work". Following the law, then, is no alien and imposed obligation, but the spontaneous desire of our heart, and therefore in living our lives of gratitude, we shall not covet anything contrary to God's commandments.

If the Heidelberg Catechism would have brought the exposition of the Ten Commandments to a close with this interpretation of covetousness as the root and cause of all sin, we might very well be tempted to give up in frustration and resignation. Who can obey all commandments perfectly in never coveting what is not his or hers? The Heidelberg Catechism with its realistic assessment of human sin and its still powerful influence on us replies quite matter-of-factly: no one, not even the holiest (question 114). But this is no reason for despair, since we are not left in the comfort-less misery of our sin. We are delivered from this misery by Christ, engrafted into him and given his Spirit, and therefore, those converted to God do really begin with a small beginning of obedience, yearning and praying for being "renewed more and more after God's image" by the Holy Spirit (question 115). Preaching the Ten Commandments has a didactic and pastoral aim: It teaches us not only "how great my sin and misery are", but also "how I am set free from all my sins and misery", to use the words of question 2. Consequently, the preaching of the Ten Commandments, according to the first use of the law, tutors us to Christ, in whom we find forgiveness of sins and righteousness, and thereby teaches us to live in the joy of our only comfort. And only by living in this comfort are we enabled to "never stop striving, and never stop praying to God for the grace of the Holy Spirit". The life of gratitude, to which the Heidelberg Catechism wants to guide us, depends on the grace of the Holy Spirit, for which we pray incessantly and confidently. It is only consequential when the Heidelberg Catechism in its last section proceeds to discuss prayer as part of our gratitude before concluding all its reflections and contemplations *on* God with actually talking *to* God in prayer.

Prayer

Lord's Day 45 (116–119): Prayer as Thankfulness

Q. 116 Why do Christians need to pray?
A. Because prayer is the most important part of the thankfulness God requires of us. And also because God gives his grace and Holy Spirit only to those who pray continually and groan inwardly, asking God for these gifts and thanking God for them.

Q. 117 What is the kind of prayer that pleases God and that he listens to?
A. First, we must pray from the heart to no other than the one true God, revealed to us in his Word, asking for everything God has commanded us to ask for. Second, we must fully recognize our need and misery, so that we humble ourselves in God's majestic presence. Third, we must rest on this unshakable foundation: even though we do not deserve it, God will surely listen to our prayer because of Christ our Lord. That is what God promised us in his Word.

Q. 118 What did God command us to pray for?
A. Everything we need, spiritually and physically, as embraced in the prayer Christ our Lord himself taught us.

Q. 119 What is this prayer?
A. Our Father in heaven, hallowed be your name. Your kingdom come. Your will be done, on earth as it is in heaven. Give us this day our daily bread. And forgive us our debts, as we also have forgiven our debtors. And do not bring us to the time of trial, but rescue us from the evil one. For the kingdom and the power and the glory are yours forever. Amen.

The Heidelberg Catechism acknowledges with answer 116 that there is indeed a need for prayer, yet attributes this need, probably against most people's expectations, not to some inner human desire for intimate relation to God in devout prayer, but to God's commandment. God requires from us to pray, and prayer is not just one, but *the most important* part of thankfulness. According to the catechism, prayer is, thus, primarily a thankful act of obedience or an obedient act of thankfulness. As we have said earlier, gratitude is our response to God's grace, and all of God's commandments serve us as a guide to live this life of gratitude in all spheres of our lives. Prayer is, first and foremost, thankful response to God's grace, because in prayer we give thanks for all God has done for us in Christ, *and* we continuously ask God for the gift of grace. In doing so, we, as those who have been delivered by God, surrender ourselves completely to this Deliverer, trusting God's promises and not ourselves, or as Karl Barth has formulated: "When I really pray, I prove just in this way the genuineness of my fear of God and confidence in him." At the same time, our prayer as thanksgiving and petition is addressed to the very God whom we may call "Father" because of Jesus Christ and who through the work of the Holy Spirit helps us to pray rightly. Prayer is based on, encompassed by, aimed at, and suffused with God's grace; it rests completely on the believer's comfort of belonging to God, *and* it promotes this comfort in the believer.

Question 117 unfolds this grace-centeredness of prayer in three aspects, describing the kind of prayer that pleases God and to which God listens; in short, those kind of prayers that follow God's good will for us. a) God's grace enables us through the work of the Holy Spirit to pray from our heart, that is, to pray honestly as those who *we really are* in our inmost person, to the one true God, that is, to who *God really is* as our Creator, Redeemer, and Sanctifier. God's grace in Christ permits us to pray to this God, our Father, who has revealed Godself in the Word, and prohibits us from praying to all substitutes of the true God, whether they are saints or human-made idols and concepts. b) Humbling ourselves in God's majestic presence, and admitting our sinful misery is, according to the structure of the Heidelberg Catechism and its triple knowledge, part of living in the joy of our only comfort (question 2), and hence is always accompanied by our faith in God's gift of grace as forgiveness of our sins. Again, we pray honestly as those who we really are: pardoned sinners, but sinners nevertheless. c) Because of Jesus Christ, our Lord and Brother, we can pray to God confidently, assured by the Holy Spirit that God will indeed listen to our prayer. There is nothing we would have to do in advance in order for our prayers to be heard by God; we cannot and need not try to earn God's favor. The unshakable foundation of prayer is grace, and we have God's word for this.

Whereas question 117 addressed *how* we are to pray – honestly, humbly, and confidently – the following question deals with the *what* of prayer. Keeping in mind what the catechism has confessed earlier concerning the providence of God (question 27: "*all things,* in fact, come to us not by chance but by his fatherly hand"), it does not come as a surprise that the Heidelberg Catechism instructs us to pray for *everything* we need, spiritually and physically, for our souls as well as for our bodies. The little word "need" should not be ignored, because it has enormous practical and spiritual consequences: we are asked and permitted to pray what for everything we really *need,* not for everything we *want.* We are called to distinguish between needing and wanting, and we are given an aid for this challenging task by Jesus Christ, who taught us his prayer – to which the Heidelberg Catechism now turns.

Lord's Day 46–52 (120–129): The Lord's Prayer

Q. 120 Why did Christ command us to call God "our Father"?
A. To awaken in us at the very beginning of our prayer what should be basic to our prayer – a childlike reverence and trust that through Christ God has become our Father, and that just as our parents do not refuse us the things of this life, even less will God our Father refuse to give us what we ask in faith.

Q. 121 Why the words "in heaven"?
A. These words teach us not to think of God's heavenly majesty as something earthly, and to expect everything needed for body and soul from God's almighty power.

Q. 122 What does the first petition mean?

A. "Hallowed be your name" means: Help us to truly know you, to honor, glorify, and praise you for all your works and for all that shines forth from them: your almighty power, wisdom, kindness, justice, mercy, and truth. And it means, Help us to direct all our living – what we think, say, and do – so that your name will never be blasphemed because of us but always honored and praised.

Q. 123 What does the second petition mean?

A. "Your kingdom come" means: Rule us by your Word and Spirit in such a way that more and more we submit to you. Preserve your church and make it grow. Destroy the devil's work; destroy every force which revolts against you and every conspiracy against your holy Word. Do this until your kingdom fully comes, when you will be all in all.

Q. 124 What does the third petition mean?

A. "Your will be done, on earth as it is in heaven" means: Help us and all people to reject our own wills and to obey your will without any back talk. Your will alone is good. Help us one and all to carry out the work we are called to, as willingly and faithfully as the angels in heaven.

Q. 125 What does the fourth petition mean?

A. "Give us this day our daily bread" means: Do take care of all our physical needs so that we come to know that you are the only source of everything good, and that neither our work and worry nor your gifts can do us any good without your blessing. And so help us to give up our trust in creatures and trust in you alone.

Q. 126 What does the fifth petition mean?

A. "Forgive us our debts, as we also have forgiven our debtors" means: Because of Christ's blood, do not hold against us, poor sinners that we are, any of the sins we do or the evil that constantly clings to us. Forgive us just as we are fully determined, as evidence of your grace in us, to forgive our neighbors.

Q. 127 What does the sixth petition mean?
A. "And do not bring us to the time of trial, but rescue us from the evil one" means: By ourselves we are too weak to hold our own even for a moment. And our sworn enemies – the devil, the world, and our own flesh – never stop attacking us. And so, Lord, uphold us and make us strong with the strength of your Holy Spirit, so that we may not go down to defeat in this spiritual struggle, but may firmly resist our enemies until we finally win the complete victory.

Q. 128 What does your conclusion to this prayer mean?
A. "For the kingdom and the power and the glory are yours forever" means: We have made all these petitions of you because, as our all-powerful king, you are both willing and able to give us all that is good; and because your holy name, and not we ourselves, should receive all the praise, forever.

Q. 129 What does that little word "Amen" express?
A. "Amen" means: This shall truly and surely be! It is even more sure that God listens to my prayer than that I really desire what I pray for.

The expositions of Decalogue and the Lord's Prayer do not actually add new theological material to what has already been discussed before in the catechism, but weave together major themes of the first two parts in a magnificent way, introducing them as applications of doctrine, as practical consequences for our life. As we have seen, these two texts are understood from the perspective of gratitude God requires from us, and both, commandments as well as petitions, aim at directing our focus always and everywhere on God and God's will for our life. What is new in the exposition of the Lord's Prayer, though, is that the doctrine developed earlier is now turned into prayer petitions in the context of the grateful life. Clearly the catechism does not know of an opposition between doctrine, piety, and action! It is thus more than adequate that the Heidelberg Catechism, known and cherished for its devotional and warm character, concludes it contemplations with turning directly to God and addressing God in prayer. Each answer to the six petitions of the Lord's Prayer is actually in itself a brief prayer, providing the congregation and the individual believer with a supportive framework for their devotional life. But before the catechism turns to the six petitions, it opens its reflections on the Lord's Prayer with a prologue discussing the expressions "Our Father" (question 120) and "in heaven" (question 121) in order to introduce the appropriate praying attitude of reverence and trust.

By grace through Jesus Christ, we are adopted children of God (question 33), and the almighty God is our faithful father (question 26); that is why Jesus Christ taught us to address God with this familial term: our Father, Abba, Daddy. Contained in this name is our relationship to God; we may and should relate to God in reverence and trust, all the time, but especially at beginning of our prayer, expecting and asking from God everything we need (question 118), in the good confidence that God will provide (question 128). And even though the Heidelberg Catechism uses the metaphor of a parent-child relationship, it still is aware that this is only a metaphor, because we are not allowed to think of "God's heavenly majesty as something earthly". God is faithful father, indeed, but God is also "exalted, mighty, incomprehensible" (Calvin's Genevan Catechism); even as children of our heavenly father, our loving relation with God is described by the first table of the law, which emphatically stresses our responsibility to truly worship God alone and not to turn God into an idol according to our perceptions and imaginings. God remains God, faithful father and almighty God, and in addressing God in our prayers as "our Father in heaven" we acknowledge this, and, at the same time, rely on God to provide us with everything we need. In this prayer attitude of reverence and trust, the six petitions of the Lord's Prayer are brought before God.

The first three of the six petitions are the so-called "thou petitions", because they refer the praying person and community immediately to God: God's name, will, and reign; whereas the following three petitions, the so-called "we petitions", are concerned with us (and not just "me"): our daily bread, debt, temptation. In that, the Lord's Prayer resembles the Ten Commandment in its twofold direction towards God and neighbor. And just like the Heidelberg Catechism assigned one commandment to one Lord's Day, so also one petition of the Lord's Prayer is assigned to one Sunday, stressing the Heidelberg Catechism's understanding of the persisting importance and significance of both traditional catechetical texts for the church's and believers' faith and life. And one more preliminary note is in order, before we turn our attention to the six petitions. We would misread the Heidelberg Catechism's interpretation of the Lord's Prayer, of all prayer indeed, if we would take the earlier mentioned "childlike reverence and trust" to mean that God's praying people passively await God's intervention without ever becoming engaged themselves in what they have prayed for. Just the opposite is true, as praying and working are intimately related in a twofold way: not only does prayer lead to responsible action, but prayer also prays for God to conform us to God's will and help us to become actively involved. Thus with each exposition of the six petitions, the Heidelberg Catechism asks for two things: "for God's helpful intervention, and then also for God's strength for corresponding intervening action on our part for God and the world" (Eberhard Busch).

According to the Heidelberg Catechism, in praying the first petition, "hallowed be your name", we ask God for help in a dual perspective: for true knowledge of God and for direction of our living. If we truly know God, who God is for us (and thus who we are for God), we respond to God's work in honoring, glorifying, and praising God. From God's work in creating, redeeming, and sanctifying us, we recognize God's almighty power, wisdom, kindness, justice, mercy, truth – those attributes of God the Heidelberg Catechism has taken great pains to explain and clarify throughout the course of its 129 questions. We cannot, however, do this by ourselves; we need God's help in directing "all our living", our thoughts, words, and deeds – the correspondence to the exposition of the third commandment (question 99) is obvious at this point. In that sense, the first petition could be understood as a prayer for the grace of the Holy Spirit, who makes us wholeheartedly willing and ready from now on to live for God (question 1), and who renews us *more and more* after God's image (question 115).

The second petition, "your kingdom come", asks God, in agreement with this line of thought, to rule us by "Word and Spirit" (as we have seen, a frequently used expression throughout the whole catechism) so that "more and more" we submit ourselves to God – until God will be fully with us and we fully with God. We are living in between the times, in the "already and not yet"; we have not yet attained perfect blessedness, but "we already now experience in our heart the beginning of eternal joy" (question 58); thus we pray confidently and comforted for God's kingdom to come, knowing that in Christ the kingdom has already come near [Mk 1:15]. This very Christ is the one who through his Spirit and Word [sic] gathers, protects, and preservers for himself a community (question 54), the church. And until God's kingdom *fully* comes, we ask for God's protection and the growth of this church; not for selfish or triumphant reasons, though – the church is in no way to be confused with the kingdom of God! Nevertheless, the church may ask, with childlike reverence and trust, to be protected and to be added to, for the sake of the true proclamation of the word to the entire world. We need God's protection, God's rule by Word and Spirit, because even though we benefit in Christ's glory as our head, in that he defends us and keeps us safe from all enemies (question 51 and 52), evil is still at work in the world and in us, conspiring against the kingdom of God, and we still have to wait for Christ's return, when God will be all in all.

At the center of the Heidelberg Catechism's exposition of the third petition, "your will be done", stands a central gospel claim and truth, which includes in itself all explications of this passage: only God's will is good. This is why we pray for God's help in order to reject our wills, or rather to mold our wills according to the will of God. Obedience to God, that means, living according to the will of God in the rising-to-life of the new self, is a love and delight (question 90). Rejecting our own corrupt will, thus, is part of our conversion and of the dying-away of the old self, in the sure belief that our will, too, is restored to the image of Christ by the grace of the Holy Spirit – and for this grace we pray with the third petition. This grace of God does not only conform our will to God's will, but also and as much helps us to accomplish the works we are called to do; it is an enabling and vitalizing grace that makes us do the good we want, and not the evil we do not want [cf. Rom 7:19].

Turning now to the "we petitions", the Heidelberg Catechism repeats from a different angle what has been said before. "Give us this day our daily bread" means not only to ask God to provide for all our bodily needs, but also to help us see that *God alone* is the source of

everything good, and thus *God alone* deserves our trust. God takes
care of something as material and earthly as our bodily needs, and
from this we may learn who God is and what we ultimately need:
God's blessing. The Heidelberg Catechism does not discard our "work
and worry", but just the opposite, as we have seen in the exposition of
the third petition and throughout the catechism in all its reflections
on "good works" (for example in questions 88–91). It emphasizes,
however, that without God's graciousness and love nothing, not even
God's own gifts, will benefit us. In praying for our daily bread, we
acknowledge our ongoing and all-encompassing dependence on God,
who will not refuse to give us what we ask in faith (question 120).

Because of "Christ's blood", Christ's sacrifice on the cross, our
sins have been forgiven as is witnessed to us exemplary in the sacraments. We therefore may ask God to "forgive us our debts", as the
sixth petition prays, even though we know ourselves to still be poor
sinners, persistently inclined to do evil. Yet by God's grace and the
work of the Holy Spirit, we just as persistently cling to God, "displeased with our sins, but nevertheless trusting that our sins are pardoned" (question 81), being "renewed and sanctified to be members
of Christ, so that more and more we become dead to sin and live
holy and blameless lives" (question 70). We have experienced God's
unmerited, sheer grace and are experiencing it anew every day, and
it is this grace that works in us and makes us "fully determined" to
forgive others *as a witness* to God's grace. We do not merit our forgiveness by first forgiving other, as if this was a precondition for God
to forgive us; in addition, God's forgiving grace is no dead deposit
in us, but a living force that opens up new avenues of grateful living
for us. In praying to God to forgive us our debts because of Christ's
blood, we actually accept God's gift of grace with a believing heart
and *are* thus righteous before God (question 60).

The sixth, and final, petition "do not bring us to the time of trial,
but rescue us from the evil one", has been counted as two in the
Lutheran and also Roman Catholic tradition, but the Heidelberg
Catechism follows Calvin in understanding it as one petition. What
do we pray with these words of the sixth petition according to the
Heidelberg Catechism? Our prayer has two parts; the first one being
actually more of a confessional "status report": we are not only sinful,

but also weak people, and we are constantly under attack of evil, all that revolts against God and God's goodness: the devil, the world, and our own flesh, that is, our own sinfulness. In times of trial, we cannot prevail on our own. We are weak, indeed, yet we are not powerless. The Lord, our all-powerful king, does not only "defend and keep us safe from all enemies" (question 51), but also sends his Spirit. And it is for this Spirit we pray, this Spirit who restores us to the image of Christ in such a way that we are strengthened and empowered to follow Jesus in praying "not my will but yours be done" [Luke 22:42], coming through this spiritual struggle with firm resistance. And even though it may not look like it at times, we can be assured that Christ has already won the final victory, and that we as members of Christ share in this victory. For this we are anointed by the Holy Spirit, and thus called "Christians": to strive with a free conscience against sin and the devil in this life, and afterward to reign with Christ over all creation for eternity (question 32).

In a beautiful way, the conclusion of the Lord's Prayer, and of the Heidelberg Catechism's exposition of it, captures and elucidates its overall intention: that God's holy name may be praised, forever. This is the catechism's purpose in each of its 129 questions, because this is the ultimate goal of all human life, this is what God has created us for in God's own image: to praise and glorify God (question 6). We praise and glorify God by asking God for everything we need, spiritually and physically, by thanking God for all gifts of grace. We praise and glorify God by assuredly trusting God alone as our all-powerful king and our loving father, who will give us all that is good, knowing that "God is able to this because he is almighty God, and desires to do this because he is a faithful Father" (question 26). And because of who God is, we can "rest on this unshakable foundation …: God will surely listen to our prayer because of Christ our Lord" (question 116). So we can finish our prayer, secure in the comfort of belonging to God, body and soul, in life and in death, with this little word "Amen" – This shall truly and surely be!

Beginning the Conversation

With "Amen", the Heidelberg Catechism concludes not only its exposition of the Lord's Prayer, but brings its instruction into the Christian faith to a close. In 129 questions, the catechism has unfolded what the first question confessed as the summary of the holy gospel: that we belong to our faithful Savior Jesus Christ. Our task, however, is not yet completed, if we are to take the Heidelberg Catechism seriously. We have endeavored to listen with respect to the catechism's understanding of the Christian faith and its implications for Christian life, yet this is only the very first step in our engagement with this 450-year old document witnessing, above all, to God's grace in Christ. Now we are called to engage in a real conversation with it, challenging what we see as problematic or possibly even as not in accord with biblical teaching, assenting to and incorporating into our faith and life what we see as conveying the gospel truth, and integrating into our proclamation what we are convinced will promote Christ, thus heeding Paul's advice to test everything and hold fast to what is good. The Heidelberg Catechism never aspired to be understood and revered as a textbook containing the eternal truth of God, but only as a commentary on Scripture to which it always wants to refer its readers. Yet the authors of the Heidelberg Catechism and numerous generations after them were convinced that their exposition of the Christian faith was not only based on the bible, but was indeed bringing to light the comfort of the gospel for the glory of God. The task of contemporary Christians, especially those within the Reformed tradition, will be to join the Heidelberg Catechism in this endeavor, answering in a comforted, confident, encouraged, and joyful way the age-old and ever new question: "But why are *you* called a Christian?"

Selected Bibliography

For quotations from the Bible the New Revised Standard Version was used.

The English translation of the Heidelberg Catechism used in this book is the new translation (2011) prepared by the *Christian Reformed Church in America,* the *Reformed Church in America,* and the *Presbyterian Church (U.S.A.),* and may be found on the following websites (last accessed on April 13, 2013):

http://images.rca.org/docs/aboutus/TheHeidelbergCatechism.pdf
http://www.crcna.org/sites/default/files/HeidelbergCatechism.pdf
http://www.pcusa.org/media/uploads/oga/pdf/amendments_220_part1.pdf

Commentaries

Barth, Karl; transl. by Guthrie, Shirley C. (1964): Learning Jesus Christ through the Heidelberg Catechism (Grand Rapids: William B. Eerdmans) [Quotations on pages 123, 122, 138, 134, 128, 71, 94, 99, 139]

Busch, Eberhard; transl. by William Rader (2010): Drawn to Freedom. Christian Faith today in Conversation with the Heidelberg Catechism (Grand Rapids: W. B. Eerdmans) [Quotations on pages 10, 20, 180, 205, 240, 241, 286–7, 310, 328, 333]

Bruggink, Donald J.; Hageman, Howard G. (1963): Guilt, Grace and Gratitude. A Commentary on the Heidelberg Catechism commemorating its 400th anniversary (New York: Half Moon Press)

Klooster, Fred H. (2001): Our Only Comfort. A Comprehensive Commentary on the Heidelberg Catechism (Grand Rapids: Faith Alive Christian Resources) [Quotations on pages 226, 740, 756, 1032]

Kuyvenhoven, Andrew (1988): Comfort & Joy. A Study of the Heidelberg Catechism (Grands Rapids: CRC Publ). [Quotation on page 14]

Verhey, Allen (1986): Living the Heidelberg. The Heidelberg Catechism and the Moral Life (Grand Rapids: CRC Publications) [Quotations on pages 12, 38, 88, 101, 101, 134]

Collections of Essays on the Heidelberg Catechism

Bierma, Lyle D. (ed.) (2005): An Introduction to the Heidelberg Catechism. Sources, History, and Theology; with a translation of the smaller and larger catechisms of Zacharias Ursinus (Grand Rapids: Baker Academic; Texts and studies in Reformation and post-Reformation thought)

Thompson, Bard (1963): Essays on the Heidelberg Catechism (Philadelphia: United Church Press)

Van't Spijker, Willem; Bilkes, Gerrit (ed.) (2008): The Church's Cook of Comfort (Grand Rapids: Reformation Heritage Books)

Writings of Particular Interest

Berkhoff, Hendrikus (1963): The Catechism as an Expression of Our Faith. In: Thompson, Bard (1963): Essays on the Heidelberg Catechism (Philadelphia: United Church Press), p. 93–122 [Quotation on page 93]

Bierma, Lyle D. (2006): The Theological Distinctiveness of the Heidelberg Catechism. In: *Theologia reformata* 49 (4), p. 331–341

Boekestein, William; Hughes, Evan (2011): The Quest for Comfort. The Story of the Heidelberg Catechism (Grand Rapids: Reformation Heritage Books)

Boerke, Christa (2008): The People behind the Heidelberg Catechism. In: W. 't van Spijker und Gerrit Bilkes (eds.): The Church's Cook of Comfort (Grand Rapids: Reformation Heritage Books), p. 62–88

Boerke, Christa (2008): The Reformation in Germany. In: W. 't van Spijker und Gerrit Bilkes (eds.): The Church's Book of Comfort (Grand Rapids: Reformation Heritage Books), p. 1–26

Calvin, John: Institutes of the Christian Religion, 2 vols., John T. McNeill (ed.), transl. by Ford Lewis Battles (Philadelphia: Westminster 1960) [quotation from II.16.6.; I.11.1]

Gunnoe, Charles D., JR. (2005): The Reformation of the Palatinate and the Origins of the Heidelberg Catechism, 1500–1562. In: Lyle D. Bierma (ed.): An Introduction to the Heidelberg Catechism. Sources, History, and Theology; with a translation of the smaller and larger catechisms of Zacharias Ursinus (Grand Rapids: Baker Academic; Texts and studies in Reformation and post-Reformation thought), p. 15–47

Guthrie, Shirley C. (1964): Translator's Preface. In: Learning Jesus Christ through the Heidelberg Catechism (Grand Rapid: William B. Eerdmans) [Quotation on page 11]

Hageman, Howard G. (1963): The Catechism in Christian Nurture. In: Bruggink, Donald J.; Hageman, Howard G. (eds.): Guilt, Grace and Gratitude. A Commentary on the Heidelberg Catechism commemorating its 400th anniversary (New York: Half Moon Press), p. 155–179 [Quotation on page 179]

Heinsius, Maria (1964): Frauen der Reformationszeit am Oberrhein (Karlsruhe: Hans Thoma)

Hesselink, I. John: The Dramatic Story of the Heidelberg Catechism. In: *Later Calvinism*. In: Graham, W. Fred (ed.) (1994): Later Calvinism. International perspectives (Kirksville: Sixteenth Century Journal Publishers), p. 273–288

Hoezee, Scott (1998): Speaking of Comfort. A look at the Heidelberg Catechism (Grand Rapids: CRC-Publ.)

Hyde, Daniel R. (2006): The Holy Spirit in the Heidelberg Catechism. In: Mid-America Journal of Theology 17 (Jan 1, 2006), p. 211–237 [Quotation on page 212 (with reference to Fred Klooster, A mighty Comfort, p. 59), 237]

Klooster Fred H. (1990): A Mighty Comfort: The Christian Faith According to the Heidelberg Catechism, (Grand Rapids: CRC Publications)

Latzel, Thorsten (2004): Theologische Grundzüge des Heidelberger Katechismus. Eine fundamentaltheologische Untersuchung seines Ansatzes zur Glaubenskommunikation (Marburg: N.G. Elwert)

McKim, Donald (2000): Westminster Dictionary of Theological Terms (Louisville: Westminster/John Knox Press)

Olevian, Caspar; Bierma, Lyle D. (1995): A Firm Foundation. An aid to interpreting the Heidelberg Catechism (Grand Rapids: Baker Books; Texts and Studies in Reformation and post-Reformation thought, 1)

Ottati, Douglas F. (2006): The Strange Logic of Grace in the Heidelberg Catechism. In: Ottati, D.: Theology for liberal Presbyterians and other endangered species (Louisville: Geneva Press), p. 34–48

Schaff, Philipp (1877): The Creeds of Christendom with a History and Critical Notes. (New York: Harper; Bibliotheca Symbolica Ecclesiae Universalis) [Quotations on pages 549, 536]

Thompson, John L. (2005): A Conversation with the Reformation Confessions. In: Joseph D. Small (ed.): Conversations with the confessions. Dialogue in the reformed tradition (Louisville: Geneva Press), p. 33–50

Ursinus, Zacharias: The Larger Catechism. In: Bierma, Lyle D. (ed.) (2005): An Introduction to the Heidelberg Catechism. Sources, History, and Theology; with a translation of the smaller and larger catechisms of Zacharias Ursinus (Grand Rapids: Baker Academic; Texts and studies in Reformation and post-Reformation thought), p. 163–223

Van't Spijker, Willem (2008): The Theology of the Heidelberg Catechism. In: Van't Spijker, W. 't; Bilkes, Gerrit (eds.) (2008): The Church's Book of Comfort (Grand Rapids: Reformation Heritage Books), p. 89–128 [Quotation on page 97]

Verboom, Wim (2008): The Completion of the Heidelberg Catechism. In: W. 't van Spijker und Gerrit Bilkes (eds.): The Church's Book of Comfort (Grand Rapids: Reformation Heritage Books), p. 27–61 [Quotation on p. 58]

Visser, Derk (Hg.) (1986): Controversy and Conciliation. The Reformation and the Palatinate, 1559–1583 (Allison Park: Pickwick Publications)

Visser, Derk (1983): Zacharias Ursinus. The Reluctant Reformer: His Life and Times (New York, United Church Press)

Working, Randal (2001): From Rebellion to Redemption. A Journey through the Great Themes of Christian faith : a year of reflections on the Heidelberg catechism (Colorado Springs: NavPress).

Online Resources

All webpages were last accessed on April 13, 2013.

Luther, Martin, Large Catechism
  http://www.ccel.org/ccel/luther/largecatechism.html
Westminster Larger Catechism
  http://www.ccel.org/ccel/anonymous/westminster2

Heidelberg Catechism: History, Resources, Topics, etc. (sponsored by the Canadian Reformed Theological Seminary)
  www.heidelberg-catechism.com
Platform for the Studies of the Heidelberg Catechism (sponsored by the Faculty of Divinity Leiden/The Netherlands)
  http://www.heidelbergsecatechismus.nl/index.php
Synod of the GKJTU (2008): Supplement on the Heidelberg Catechism
  http://www.heidelberger-katechismus.net/daten/File/Upload/PKH1–04In-donesiaDeutschEnglish.pdf
Ursinus, Zacharias: What is Catechism? (This article is found at the beginning of his commentary on the Heidelberg Catechism under the heading, "Special prolegomena with reference to the catechism")
  http://www.ccel.org/ccel/ursinus/catechism.txt
Weinrich, Michael (2013): Vermittlung gescheitert: Ein Rückblick auf 450 Jahre Heidelberger Katechismus. In: EKD, Schatten der Reformation: Der lange Weg zur Toleranz, p. 22–24
  http://www.kirche-im-aufbruch.ekd.de/images/Toleranzmagazin_Endfassung.pdf

Macht des Glaubens –
450 Jahre
Heidelberger Katechismus

Hrsg. im Auftrag von Refo500 von
Karla Apperloo-Boersma und
Herman J. Selderhuis.
2013. 460 Seiten mit ca. 700 Abb.,
gebunden
ISBN 978-3-525-55048-9

Power of Faith - 450 Years
of the Heidelberg Catechism

Edited on behalf of Refo500 by
K. Apperloo-Boersma and
H.J. Selderhuis.
2013. 454 pp incl. ca. 700 illustra-
tions, hardcover
ISBN 978-3-525-55049-6

Die bedeutendste Bekenntnisschrift der reformierten Kirche
prägt seit 1563 das Leben vieler Gläubigen auf allen Konti-
nenten. Mehr als 700 eindrucksvolle Bilddokumente und die
Beiträge verschiedener Fachleute beschreiben diesen Sieges-
zug!

This major protestant confession influenced the everyday life
on all continents since 1563. More than 250 illustrations and
the contributes of several specialists paint an impressive picture of this triumph!

Vandenhoeck & Ruprecht

Was heißt es, Christ zu sein?

V&R

Georg Plasger

Glauben heute mit dem Heidelberger Katechismus

2012. 212 Seiten mit 1 Abb., geb.
ISBN 978-3-525-55044-1
E-Book ISBN 978-3-647-55044-2

Kann ein Text aus dem 16. Jahrhundert auch im 21. Jahrhundert noch aktuell sein? Der Heidelberger Katechismus von 1563 scheint seine Bedeutung für die Gegenwart verloren zu haben. Georg Plasger beweist, dass der Heidelberger Katechismus auch knapp ein halbes Jahrtausend nach seiner Entstehung hilft, aktuelle Glaubensfragen zu beantworten. Mithilfe des alten Textes erläutert Plasger elementare Grundthemen des christlichen Glaubens. So entsteht eine aktuelle Glaubenslehre für jeden, der seinen Glauben besser verstehen möchte.

Vandenhoeck & Ruprecht